Advance Reviews of The Ha Ha's of Effective Relationships

In this fast-paced telling of Alex's self-discovery, Dr. Prince helps us to understand how we are perceived by others and why; why we view others' behaviors as we do; and techniques that can be used to improve our interactions and build better relationships. Prince's sharing of his vast experience with a wide-spectrum of individuals enables us to gain invaluable insights that can lead to our becoming much more competent, productive and successful human beings.

Pat Smith, Former president of Ohio
Board of Education and Educational
Policy Advisor to the Ohio Office of
Budget and Management

This is a must read business book that Gerald Prince has cleverly put into an enjoyable story. The reader will come to realize the importance of relationships in business and in life and will discover the elusive skills crucial to building these relationships.

Dimon McFerson,
Chairman and CEO,
Nationwide Insurance and Nationwide Financial Services (retired)

The "Ah Ha's" of Effective Relationships offers a fantastic story of understanding and appreciation for the strengths and weaknesses of the various personality styles. Alex's story helped me to understand and to value important ideas that at first hearing I might have rejected. The strategies for communicating with versatility that recognize the unique preferences of each style are just what I needed to hear. This book is equally important in business and in personal relationships. I highly recommend, The "Ah Ha's" of Effective Relationships.

George Norris, DVM
Junior Chamber of Commerce's Businessman of the Year
Past President, Ohio Veterinarian Medical Association

The Ah Ha's of Effective Relationships is a must read for anyone wishing to improve their interpersonal relationships. We know who we are and why we do the things we do intuitively, and the book sheds a whole new light on giving our "personalities" a face. This book is a definite supplement to my leadership coaching practice.

Glenn Furuya,
President,
Leadership Works,
A Hawaii based leadership development and consulting firm.

In the more than 30 years that I have been involved in providing executive coaching and leadership development services I have come across many great and useful bodies of knowledge. I would rank the principles presented by Dr. Prince in "The 'Ah Ha's' of Effective Relationships" to be the most practical and successful of any I have experienced for getting outstanding results with and through others while minimizing their stress. Dr. Prince does a brilliant job of introducing, building upon, and interrelating a comprehensive set of powerful influencing principles, all in the context of a very captivating executive development case study. Great principles! Great examples! Great story! Great book!

Denis W. Stoddard Ph.D.
President,
Stoddard and Associates, Ltd.

The "Ah Ha's" of Effective Relationships

The "Ah Ha's" of Effective Relationships

Gerald L. Prince

iUniverse, Inc.
New York Lincoln Shanghai

The "Ah Ha's" of Effective Relationships

iUniverse books may be ordered through booksellers or by contacting:

iUniverse
2021 Pine Lake Road, Suite 100
Lincoln, NE 68512
www.iuniverse.com
1-800-Authors (1-800-288-4677)

ISBN-13: 978-0-595-36440-4 (pbk)
ISBN-13: 978-0-595-80872-4 (ebk)
ISBN-10: 0-595-36440-3 (pbk)
ISBN-10: 0-595-80872-7 (ebk)

Printed in the United States of America

Contents

ACKNOWLEDGEMENTS

Many individuals have assisted in and encouraged the writing of this book about how interactions between people can be mutually satisfying and produce positive results. Friends and colleagues, who have participated in the hundreds of seminars and numerous coaching situations, provided the seeds that grew into this story. The most significant help came from my wife, Barbara. Without her endless patience, encouragement, suggestions, and corrections, this book would not have been possible.

The SOCIAL STYLE MODEL comes from the original research and study of David Merrill and Roger Reid. The TRACOM Corporation markets and continues the work using the SOCIAL STYLE MODEL. John Myers, the President of The TRACOM Corporation, has provided helpful suggestions.

INTRODUCTION

The "Ah Ha's" of Effective Relationships will help you understand and meet the challenge of interacting effectively with the people who are important in your life. You will travel with Alex Boden as he learns that his own success depends directly on how well he develops effective relationships.

Interacting with other people, so that real communication occurs, is one of the greatest challenges we face, particularly when problems arise. We hope we can come to mutually agreeable solutions, and we are pleased when we feel that our efforts are rewarded, when effective interaction comes naturally and easily. But communication too often fails when we believe that everyone interacts with others in the same way that we do. People don't. Some listen; others talk. Some share plans; others share feelings. Some move and talk fast; others are slower to respond. We all need to learn that adjusting to different styles of interaction is crucial to effective communication and productive relationships.

Alex's story is of his journey as he finds his world turned upside down when employer, Rivonia Technology, merges with another company. There is a good chance that he will lose his job as a sales manager, so Alex decides to change careers. He begins his search by utilizing the career counseling service provided as part of his severance package.

Jan Omizo, an insightful career counselor, asks Alex to examine carefully how successful people work with and develop the talents of others. She assigns Alex a board of directors. Smokey, the chairperson of Alex's board, is the CEO of a large company. Rachel is the owner and trusted veterinarian in a bustling animal hospital, Greg is a dedicated and caring middle-school principal, Jim is an owner of a thriving antiques store, and Lonnie is a powerful and well respected local attorney.

Alex first meets with Smokey. Smokey shows Alex how the top line to success (relationships) relates to the bottom line of success (profits). Alex always knew the importance of profit and was comfortable pushing people to make money for the company, but he was not comfortable developing relationships; he did not see how doing so related to his being successful in business or life.

Alex gains many "Ah Ha's" as a result of his visits with Smokey and his board members. Smokey provides him with a unique description of how people relate to each other. The concept, that people want and need to be approached differently, is hard for Alex to grasp. This is a blind spot for him.

Though each member of Alex's board is successful in his or her particular field of work, Alex finds it difficult to accept that he can learn something from people who have jobs that are fundamentally different from his. He reluctantly visits, observes, and talks individually with his board members; he sees Rachel spending valuable time talking to clients about who has the best tomatoes in their garden. He is frustrated as he watches Greg let his staff make important decisions. He finds it strange that, though each one is a successful professional, problems still arise. Jim gives too much information about an antique brooch and almost loses a sale. Alex watches Lonnie become irritated with an intern not following directions that she had given her. He is frustrated when board members don't act the way he thinks they should act and when they don't focus on the bottom line, profit.

Alex struggles as he considers why he should change the way he works with subordinates and colleagues. Gradually, through Smokey's coaching and teaching, Alex begins to see how his board members adjust their actions to assure they build and maintain productive relationships. He begins to understand that relationships must benefit both people if any relationship is to be profitable and successful.

THIS CAN'T BE HAPPENING TO ME

Everyone thinks of changing the world,
but no one thinks
of changing himself.
—Leo Tolstoy

A pending takeover. It started with rumors, then a briefing from management that there were serious talks and Rivonia Technology could be sold in the near future. Now it was official. It had just been announced that the sale of Rivonia Technology to an international company, The Essex Group, had taken place.

What would this mean for Alex Boden? He had always been a top salesperson for Rivonia Technology; he relocated to accommodate the company, accepted a position in the regional office, and assumed management responsibility for a group that had a very average sales record. At the time, Alex felt he had been set up for failure; however, after two years, his sales group was rated second in the company, and the regional manager had recognized the improved sales in Alex's annual evaluation.

Alex was well educated. He was graduated from Miami University with a BS in business. He had always been loyal to Rivonia and served them wherever they needed help, even when it meant making personal sacrifices. The moves he made for the company created major life changes—taking his wife and kids away from grandparents, aunts, uncles, schools, and a comfortable community. Given all of this, Alex wondered, "Why would they let someone like me go?"

Alex was in his late forties, tall and handsome, with a classic chiseled face. Taking care of his appearance had always been a high priority for Alex. But recently, the lack of exercise and a poor diet had added pounds to his waistline. He had been eating fast-food lunches, so he could devote more time to his workload at Rivonia. The continued stress and additional pounds had taken a toll, and he knew it. Alex, who had always been highly involved in community and church activities, had almost stopped volunteering and participating in activities outside work.

The rumor mill was working overtime. Everyone was wondering how many existing supervisors would still be needed. Alex's concern was whether he would be kept or viewed as excess in the new company. After all, it was the same old slogan: Do more with less! The acquisition will help us to be more efficient!

Good news and bad news. The time line for making personnel decisions was announced to the sales force and the sales managers. The reorganization plan would be released in thirty days. It was good to know when the uncertainty would be over, but thirty days seemed like a long time to think and to wonder.

The next month had the potential of being the longest in Alex's life, as he attempted to sort through his feelings and options. Alex wondered what to tell his family. He had always been a private and decisive person, but this event would affect his whole family.

Leaving work that day, Alex took the long way home as he thought about what he would say. His wife, Linda, daughter, Stephanie, and son, Mitch, all led full lives and had stresses of their own. Nevertheless, it was something they needed to know.

Maybe he shouldn't tell them anything until he knew the details for sure. He wondered, "Would that be fair to them?" Facing a dilemma like this was certainly a new experience!

Suddenly, Alex was jarred back to reality; he had to be at the kids' baseball game. He was one of their coaches, and the game would be starting in less than an hour. Alex enjoyed being their coach and was proud watching his kids play. Besides, being at the game would take his mind off his job.

Mitch and Stephanie played on the same team of twelve-to fourteen-year-olds. Stephanie was one of two girls on the team and played second base. She was a real competitor and reminded Alex of himself. Athletics had always been her strength. She was a tall, slender girl, with short hair made blonder by the sun. Stephanie was a year younger than Mitch and had a Julia Roberts' smile that lit up any room she entered. She was filled with energy and could hardly wait until she was old enough to go out for the high school cross-country and basketball teams. She was even considering trying out for the boys' baseball team instead of the girls' softball team.

Mitch was a terrific baseball pitcher, more easy-going than Stephanie and less competitive, like his mother. Mitch was more a student of the game of baseball. Studying the hitters and calculating how to pitch to each batter was exciting to Mitch. His studious manner on the baseball field was the same in school and at home. Mitch was fourteen years old, muscular, yet slim, and tall for his age. He had unruly red-brown hair and liked to keep it in a stylish short cut. He was not as hyperactive as Stephanie and preferred reading over always being on the go.

The game was over too fast, and Alex was thrust back into the reality of deciding how much to share with his family. All the way home, he talked constantly to Stephanie and Mitch about the game in order to avoid talking about his job.

Mitch suggested, "Let's stop and get pizza for dinner."

Alex knew that would be a good idea because Linda was having a busy day at her school. She had just re-entered the job market after being at home for the last twelve years with their children. Linda was discovering that catching up on the new curriculums and the special needs of her students and developing relationships with the other teachers and the students' parents was difficult, but she considered it an exhilarating part of her job. She was highly committed to being an outstanding teacher.

Once Alex reached home, he greeted Linda with a hug and hurried to change his clothes. He returned to the kitchen and sat at the counter as Stephanie and Mitch dished up the pizza. As they finished eating, Alex made up his mind. This was as good a time as ever to tell them what was happening.

"As you may have heard on the news today, Rivonia was purchased by a company called The Essex Group. I don't know what this will mean to my job," Alex blurted out, his face set in a worried expression.

There were shocked looks on the faces of his family, and he realized he might have dumped a load on them without any information. Alex stopped and tried to explain more fully the situation at Rivonia. He explained that the new company would be consolidating some of the jobs. He wouldn't know what would happen with his job for at least thirty days.

Linda, Stephanie, and Mitch had questions and comments about the company. After a discussion that went much longer than Alex normally found comfortable, he felt better. His family was supportive, and he knew they understood the situation as well as could be expected.

Alex, trying to reassure them, forcefully added, "I don't need Rivonia. I can get a job with another company that will appreciate my hard work and dedication." He felt sure that he hadn't completely been able to mask the edge of distress in his voice.

After dinner, Linda sat down beside Alex and asked him if he wanted to talk more about his job. Her amber-colored eyes had assumed a tender expression. Alex didn't think he wanted to talk more, but he appreciated Linda's concern.

Linda had always been Alex's best friend since he first met her while in college. Short in stature with skin that reminded Alex of porcelain and hair that bounced when she walked, Linda was reasonably trim, but for as long as Alex had known her she had been on a diet. She had a mystical quality about her; people were magnetically drawn to her. With her friendly, inviting, and nonjudgmental manner, Linda had always made Alex feel comfortable talking to her about anything.

Gradually Alex opened up and began talking about some of the frustrations he felt with his current work and job. Linda was a good listener. She shared that she had noticed he had lost some of the passion he had always had for his work.

Alex looked surprised and said, "Is it that evident? Work has been less enjoyable for me. I don't know what it is. I don't know if it's because I don't see any possibility for advancement, or if it's that my work just doesn't excite or challenge me anymore."

Alex and Linda continued to talk for over an hour. Talking helped Alex to focus on what he really wanted from a job, on what it was that brought him the passion he had slowly lost.

After a restless night of kicking sheets and blankets, Alex rose early, saw Linda off to work, drove the kids to school, and ran some errands. He had scheduled this day as a vacation day several weeks ago, and it was a good thing, because he needed the time to think!

As hard as he tried, he couldn't keep his mind off his talk with Linda. She had raised some good questions. Did he even like what he was doing at Rivonia?

Suddenly a thought came to him like a lightning bolt. He even said it out loud. "Now is the time for change! What time could be better?" Alex had always prided himself on being decisive and in charge of what happened to him. Why not change careers, instead of waiting for some new company to make that decision? Why return to a job that he was unhappily going to each day?

Alex couldn't wait to call Linda and tell her what he was going to do. After all, Linda had helped him to see that even if the new company wanted him to continue working at his current job, it wasn't what he wanted.

Linda seemed sincerely happy and supportive when Alex told her of his decision. He appreciated her encouragement, although he had no idea where he was going to get a job.

Alex immediately called his supervisor, Virginia Hall, and set up an appointment to talk with her that afternoon. When he entered Virginia's office, Alex felt the tension of being at work again. He hadn't realized that work had been such a drain of his energy level.

Alex told Virginia that he wasn't going to wait for the new company's decision. He would take the buyout offered and leave immediately. Virginia accepted his decision and told Alex it was probably best for him.

The next few days seemed a blur; there were so many ups and downs and confusing emotions. He wondered what Virginia meant by saying that his leaving was probably the best decision. He felt hurt, even angry, that Rivonia Technology hadn't appreciated his years of hard work and loyalty.

It came down to two choices. He could sit there, feeling hurt and angry, or he could find a job. Rivonia was offering a severance package, which would provide a financial payoff and professional guidance in a job search. But where would he start? He didn't even have a current resume. He hadn't had to look for a job in so long. What types of work could he do that would restore the passion for work that he had once felt?

After a few days the initial shock wore off, and Alex began to seriously consider his options. As part of Rivonia's severance plan, he was offered outplacement counseling, a hard thing for Alex to accept, but he swallowed his pride and made an appointment for Tuesday morning. After all, Rivonia would be paying for it.

Alex awoke early, dressed, checked the address, and set out to find the outplacement center that was supposed to help him. After the frustration of looking for a parking place, he found that the office was brightly decorated but didn't seem to be very businesslike. Alex wondered what he had gotten himself into. He'd never had to get help from anyone. To make things worse, he was kept waiting fifteen minutes for his appointment.

Jan Omizo, a petite Japanese American, was the counselor assigned to direct Alex's job search efforts. Jan appeared to be in her mid-thirties. Alex had learned from the receptionist that Jan was a Pilates instructor in her free time, and she did seem to be in excellent physical condition. Alex impatiently wondered how Jan could possibly be of any help. She couldn't possibly understand the stress involved in changing careers at this stage in his life. "Well," he thought with resignation, "Jan's consult is free, and I have nothing scheduled until this afternoon."

Jan had a boatload of questions for Alex. She asked about his skills in a number of areas. What about his job did he like best? When did he feel that he was contributing the most to the company? How effective were his listening skills? Did he feel he had leadership skills? How did he develop relationships with people? Did he have a recent resume? On and on—it was all Alex could do to keep from walking out. He didn't want to waste time answering all the questions. He just wanted to find a job that he would enjoy. Enough questions!

After about twenty minutes, Alex had had enough. He interrupted Jan and huffed, "What are you thinking by taking all my time with meaningless talk? All I want are leads on jobs that will challenge me, jobs where I can be successful! Can you help me or not?"

This behavior was consistent with what Jan had learned about Alex. Jan had expected him to be impatient. She knew that at some point he would attempt to take charge of the interview. She listened carefully in order to understand his frustration with changing careers, with her, with the whole process, and with not being in control of what was happening to him.

Jan had spent a good deal of time researching background information on Alex. She was well aware that he was going to be an interesting challenge. He seemed to have been successful as a salesperson with Rivonia Technology, selling a highly technical line of merchandise for medical research. His customer relations seemed good. Clients were loyal to him, and they appreciated his honesty, his on-time delivery of products and his follow-through with the promises he made.

As a sales manager Alex had produced a turnaround in sales when he took over supervision of a low-producing region. The sales personnel immediately brought in new accounts and larger repeat orders. Sales shot up, and the region seemed to experience a sense of rejuvenation. However, with closer investigation, Jan found that four of the five sales people who had worked for Alex had either transferred to other departments or left the company within the last year. Alex's sales group had shown no gain in sales in the last two quarters, and they had lost some key accounts.

Through her research, Jan was able to gather material that indicated that Alex was a demanding supervisor, closely monitoring his salespeople and their accounts. When sales were not as expected, Alex was quick to confront and demand explanations. This strategy was effective initially, when the region was disorganized and the sales personnel weren't overly competent. As the sales force became better educated concerning its product line, the staff became more self-sufficient, and as time went on, Alex's style of dominating and directing became stifling.

He was referred to as bottom-line-Alex by his staff. The other sales managers disliked their monthly meeting because it seemed like everything was brain surgery with Alex. All things needed to be done immediately and done the way Alex thought was best. His staff saw him as being extremely opinionated and not hesitant to express his thoughts on most subjects. His agenda had to be first. Amazingly, Alex seemed unaware of how others saw him.

Because Jan had expected Alex's reaction, she stayed focused on her goal to help him. She had to think fast to keep him from becoming more upset. Jan knew that Alex respected power and position, and she had carefully designed a plan that would allow Alex to control his own investigation for seeking a meaningful career change.

"Alex, do you have a board of directors?" she responded to Alex's demand for answers.

The question caught Alex off guard, and he bluntly answered, "Companies have boards of directors; individuals don't. No, I don't. What would I do with a board of directors?"

Alex wasn't a CEO; he didn't even have a job. "Being on my board of directors would be pretty boring right now," Alex thought. He had always known what needed to be done, never relying on others for thoughts or advice.

Jan ignored Alex's frustration and went on to explain, "Receiving guidance from a board of directors is a strategy that I've found to be very useful to an individual in your position, Alex. Boards of directors sit in counsel with CEOs of businesses all the time. Their role is to consider plans for present and future situations, to give the CEO advice on the pros and cons of proceeding. In your case, the board of directors won't make the decisions, but its members will be there as trusted advisors and coaches as you consider changes in your career."

Alex stared in disbelief as Jan continued, "Your board of directors will guide you to be aware of different strategies that will help you to be more effective as a manager and as a person. They'll be looking out for your good, being honest with you when you need to hear specifics for improving your chances of being successful in various jobs. They'll serve as your coaches to help you examine your strengths and weaknesses and to suggest new skills you'll need to be competitive in the current market-place. "Your board of directors won't be a formal body, meeting together, but it will be a network of individuals with whom you'll meet one-on-one."

Jan continued quickly, leaving not one second for Alex to comment. "You'll have one board member who will serve as the chairperson. That person will coordinate your interactions and serve as a personal coach to help you understand what you're experiencing. Your chairperson will assist as you discover new insights into yourself and others. He or she will coach you to apply your new knowledge.

"Members of your Board will be carefully, specifically, chosen to help you to understand and to achieve the interpersonal skills you'll need to obtain in order to make a successful career change.

"The individuals I'll choose for your board of directors will be people who are very successful in their own fields. Some have made career changes themselves. After getting to know you, they'll help you to explore possible career choices."

If there was one thing that Alex needed, Jan thought, it was constant feedback on how people at work saw him. He needed to become aware of how his behavior affected getting tasks accomplished before he could even consider a career change. In addition, Jan knew it was essential that Alex have the opportunity to observe good role models in order to understand clearly how to be more effective himself.

While planning for this meeting, Jan had come up with the names of several successful individuals that she knew currently demonstrated and were aware of effective styles of behavior. If Alex observed and interacted with these individuals and received the same feedback from each one, he might eventually accept the idea that there were necessary changes he needed to make. He would understand the need to change, but only when he saw how changing would help him. And he was not, Jan knew, going to accept the need for changing his behavior from her. Alex appeared to need to be hit by a train for her even to get his attention.

After a few minutes considering the idea, Alex concluded that it wasn't such a bad idea. At least there would be some action. Someone actually might do something to help him. Anything would be better than just sitting and talking. It was obvious that Jan wasn't going to be of any help. Maybe this board of directors would have a few ideas. Anyway, he knew he could put up with anything for a while if the end result would be an enjoyable and productive career.

Shaking his head, Alex stood up and said, "Okay, Jan, let's try this board of directors thing you believe I need."

Jan smiled and sat forward in her chair. "I still have to do some research to find the people who will be just right to assist you. This will take me a few days. Then I'll set up appointments with each member of your board and explain to him or to her what you'll be expecting and how they may help you.

"It's important for you to spend time observing the members of your board. Watch how they work and interact with others and listen carefully to what they say. Understanding how each one has become and remains successful is essential. In addition, Alex, I want you to keep notes of what you think and feel about your observations with each member of your board."

Alex left Jan's office thinking it was strange for her to make such a big deal of the point that he needed to listen carefully and take notes. He thought, "What's her problem? Getting a job is what's important. That's what we should be talking about. I always understand what people are saying. I'm a damn good listener!" Alex bristled.

A CAST OF CHARACTERS

What do we live for,
if it is not to make life
less difficult for each other.
—George Eliot

After a few days, Jan's assistant called Alex to set up an appointment. Jan wanted to let Alex know who would be serving on his board. When Alex arrived, Jan was ready and moved right to the point. "One of the people you'll be working with is a middle school principal, Greg Drydon. Greg is in his mid-forties, was a teacher for eight years and has been a principal for about ten. As a principal Greg established himself as a steady, creative leader. He continues to support numerous successful, innovative programs. Through his empowerment and encouragement, Greg proactively worked with a large group of previously apathetic teachers, guiding and helping them to renew their passion for teaching. He consistently works with students to help them to become more involved with their own education. Through his tenacious efforts, his students' achievement levels have significantly improved."

Surprised at not being interrupted by Alex, Jan continued, "Greg has built strong relationships with his staff, students, and parents. Each group will help him with anything that he needs. His school has won national recognition for high performance and overall quality of its programs, and his students consistently score high on national, state, and local tests.

"Greg is a nurturer who has learned there are many decisions to be made, and he's aware that everyone will not always agree on the decided outcomes. It's been hard, but he has learned to take the tough stand, to work through the hard feelings with students, staff, and parents, and to build and maintain good relationships with people, yet he still gets the job done."

When Alex heard about Greg, his first reaction was anger, but he bit his lip and remained quiet. He thought, "What can a school principal possibly offer me? A middle school principal only has to keep those hormone-driven kids in school." It seemed obvious to Alex that Greg's only job was to make sure that teachers taught what they were supposed to teach and that students were made to behave and to learn.

Alex sat with clenched teeth as thoughts and questions ran rampant in his head: "Is this convoluted story of a board of directors and effective relationships just another time-wasting activity? Maybe Jan is being paid by the hour to help me. Running a school is nothing like managing a department—with all the personality quirks of the staff and the demanding customers. There's no way that a school principal can possibly understand the quick pace, the aggressive staff, and the high stress level of the business world."

Undaunted by Alex's facial expression, Jan went on to describe the next member of Alex's board. She said, "Jim Watson, an antiques entrepreneur, will be the second member of your board. Jim is acknowledged as one the most successful antique dealers in the business because of his honesty and his meticulous attention to detail. The antique business has a reputation for deceiving uninformed clients, yet Jim has built his reputation on his integrity. He assures and guarantees each antique piece that he sells to be authentic, exactly as it's described.

"Jim appreciates and thrives on the facts and history of each antique piece, though he sometimes assumes that his customers also want all this detailed information. He has become more tuned-in to his clients' needs over the years, and he's now a better judge of how much information his clients really want; he knows when the excitement of owning the piece is all that the buyer needs or wants.

"Customers come from long distances to buy from Jim. He has many loyal repeat customers because of his honesty, knowledge, and his excellence in meeting the needs of his clients."

"Antiques!" Alex thought. "How in the world can a person who sells antiques help me make a career change? At least Jim is in a business, but it's such a different business, not one that requires the technical skills that I need to have. Jim can't possibly have experienced the problems or product challenges that I've had."

Jan forced a half smile and forged ahead with her description of the next member of Alex's board of directors. "Rachel Williams is a veterinarian who operates a small animal hospital. Rachel has built a highly successful practice over the last twenty years; she has developed a loyal clientele. Her hospital is comprised of three other doctors and fifteen support staff. The veterinarians and staff have a great deal of autonomy and job responsibility for assuring that the hospital functions well.

"Rachel's enthusiasm for veterinary medicine, the pleasure her service brings to people, and the quality of her staff have made her animal hospital well-known for its innovative practices and customer satisfaction. Her staff is continually trained with new skills to better meet her clients' needs. Rachel takes pride in her high energy and the positive relationships that she has with her staff, clients, and the community. She's known as a risk taker. However, she sometimes overlooks the details. Not being detail oriented has gotten her into trouble from time to time."

Ignoring the drumming of Alex's fingers on the table, Jan summarized by saying, "Rachel has learned to temper her excitement from years of experience. She knows that she can sometimes be overwhelming to the people around her. She's learning to present her information, ideas, and enthusiasm in various ways in order to motivate people more effectively. Rachel's practice brings her a high degree of satisfaction."

As Jan continued, she watched Alex's expression, expecting steam to come from his ears at any time.

Alex was thinking, "Do you have anything at all to tell me that will be useful? Do you expect me to learn something from an animal doctor? A career change is one thing, but this is absurd! First a baby sitter! Then a junk dealer! Now a pet lover! Ridiculous!"

Jan wasn't sure how much longer she could put up with Alex's attitude. She said, "Lonnie Phillips, a local trial attorney, is the fourth member of your board. She has built her success and reputation on being a top negotiator and an attorney who welcomes big challenges. Her work is fast-paced. She drives home a point with a jury or a judge in a firm, direct style. Although she attacks most situations with the hard trial-attorney approach, Lonnie has outstanding relationships with her clients, colleagues, and the judges.

"Lonnie has had to learn that people can't be forced. Over the years, she's found that by taking time to understand people she can better help her clients and more successfully communicate with the judges, other attorneys, and juries. Lonnie is aware that some people see her as being formal and controlling. She has learned that she will be more effective with others if she brings a balance to the relationships, allowing her personal side to show through."

Alex could feel his face getting hot. He burst out in anger, "Why have you assembled such a cast of characters for my board of directors? They can't possibly help me get a job I'd be interested in. Other than having only one head, we have nothing in common!"

To himself, Alex thought, "Is Jan just pulling this stuff out of thin air?"

Undaunted, Jan calmly asked, "Alex, do you know what the top line to success is?"

"I've never heard of it, but I know the bottom line to success is hard work, knowing the product line, and making a profit!"

Top Line to Success:
Relationships, relationships,
relationships, all there is, are
relationships.

"One more to go," Jan thought thankfully. She said, "Smokey Clement, the fifth member of your board, will introduce you to the top line to success: Relationships, relationships, relationships, all there is are relationships. Positive relationships must be established and maintained if you're going to be successful in any job that deals with people. Most often, if the relationship isn't there, the customer will change to a competitor and won't even tell you what's wrong. Developing a relationship where there is trust will be invaluable as you work through the misunderstandings that will always come up."

"An interesting idea," Alex thought. "But what does this have to do with my career change?"

"Alex, if you really want to, you will learn a great deal from these individuals, especially from the fifth member of your team. Smokey Cleament is perhaps the most significant member of your board. He will have tremendous insight into what it takes to get and to keep a job like the one you hope to have."

"At last, we're getting somewhere," Alex blurted out loud.

It took all the strength Jan could muster to keep from reacting to Alex's constant pressure and impatience. She thought, "Doesn't he see how he'll come across to people during interviews and on the job? Doesn't he know that his colleagues and managers will feel that he wants to control the agenda constantly?" Jan found it hard to believe that someone like Alex was in a position of responsibility for motivating and developing a regional sales force. Jan felt that Alex must be totally unaware of how to get the best results from others without using intimidation. She thought, "A career change to anything other than a prison guard will take a major overhaul of Alex's approach."

With a great deal of control in her voice, Jan steadily moved ahead. "Smokey is to be the chairperson of your board, and he'll direct your explorations as you consider career options. He's CEO of a large company, a former mayor, a member of the hospital board, and currently a representative on several commissions for the governor. Smokey's experience in business and community service is significant, and he knows most of the CEOs in this city.

"You're fortunate, because Smokey is retiring soon, and he has agreed to assist you. He's a substantially unique individual and an excellent communicator; he's able to understand not only what is said, but also what isn't said. This ability of his may make you uncomfortable at times, since it makes you think about what you're doing and how you will affect others. He'll be an excellent coach to talk you through any concerns that you may encounter and to help you review any observations that you'll make while working with the other members of your board.

"Smokey will meet you at nine on Thursday morning at his home. First, he'll want to get to know you. Then he'll arrange and set up your schedule to observe each member on your board." Jan sighed and waited.

Alex was almost speechless. He was acquainted with Smokey from reading the newspapers and seeing him at various functions. Alex had an enormous respect for Smokey and all that he had accomplished in the business world and in service to his community. Getting a chance actually to talk with and to receive advice from Smokey was beyond any expectation Alex had ever imagined. He wondered why a person of Smokey's stature would bother to help him with a career change. Should he feel honored? Or was Smokey taking him on as a service project?

"Thanks," Alex said quietly, as he gathered his thoughts.

Alex found his voice and hesitantly but sincerely said, "It is fantastic to get a chance to meet and talk to Smokey, and maybe the other members of my board will also be of some help."

"Well, that comment is a good first step," Jan thought, as Alex stood to leave the office.

CAN THIS WORK OUT

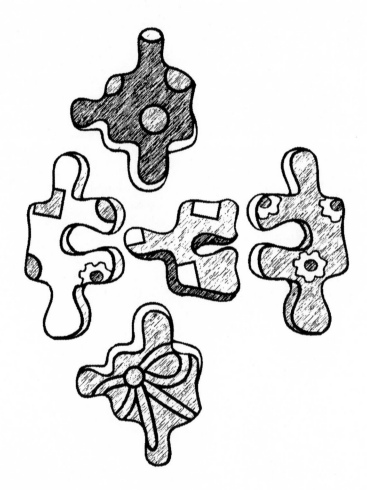

Versatility is not an act;
it's a habit practiced every day.
—Gerald L. Prince

Thursday morning at nine on the dot, Alex arrived at Smokey's home. This was an opportunity he wasn't going to miss. Alex had spent the last several days going over the questions he wanted to ask Smokey. He definitely wanted Smokey's ideas on what new and exciting careers were possibilities. Alex knew that Smokey was well respected in the community and had influence with those who did the hiring for most of the companies in town.

"Jan did something right!" Alex thought. "The opportunity to have Smokey Cleament coach me while I'm changing careers is a minor miracle. Finding a great, new career is a given now."

As Alex rang the doorbell, he felt a sense of confidence and a feeling that things were finally turning his way. He would probably have some good ideas before he left Smokey's house.

Smokey answered the door and invited Alex into his den. Smokey appeared to be about sixty-five years old; he was of medium height and walked with a slight limp, as if he had arthritis in his left knee. He was well dressed, informally, with a black sport jacket, an open-necked white shirt, gray pants, and shoes so well shined Alex could have seen his reflection. Smokey's hair was mostly gray with a trace of auburn. His eyes were hazel and he carried glasses that appeared to be for reading. Smokey had a grandfatherly smile that helped Alex feel like it was okay for him to be there.

After a few minutes of small talk, Smokey said, "You're probably wondering why I've agreed to be on your board of directors as your chairperson."

Alex, still a little overwhelmed about even being with Smokey, answered, "I don't know why you've agreed to help me, but I'll certainly appreciate anything you can do to assist me. I know I'm well qualified and I would be an asset to any company that could use my talents. I'm a hard worker, loyal, and willing to learn." Alex added a laugh that he felt was reassuring.

"Now that you mention it, why are you willing to help me?" Alex asked, wearing the question on his face.

"Well, Alex," Smokey said, "helping people to find careers where they will contribute to their company and gain personal satisfaction has long been an interest of mine. After over forty years of experience in business, I firmly believe that people will succeed only to the degree that they enjoy their work and are able to build productive relationships with others. Many individuals along the way have helped me to be more effective when interacting with others. It's my pleasure to pass this knowledge on to you."

"Well! I've never thought of relationships as being important to my success in business. I've always thought selling the product was the top priority," Alex said, shaking his head.

"Jan feels that you're motivated and that you have a lot of talent, and she wants me to be the chairperson on your board of directors. If Jan thinks I can help, and if you're a person who wants to make a positive difference, I'm willing to share what I know with you."

Alex was shocked to think that Jan thought he was a person with talent, that he could make a difference. He didn't think much of Jan, and yet she seemed to think he had the ability to be a good supervisor.

"Alex, I have about forty-five minutes before my next meeting. I want you to consider some things that will help me to better understand you and your motivation. First, I want you to gather information from your former sales staff and your regional manager at Rivonia. This information will help me to understand you through the eyes of people who have worked with you on an everyday basis. It will help me to know your style of leadership and how you adapt to different people and situations.

"For me to gather the feedback I'll need to have in order to help me understand how you work with others, I want you to give these information sheets to five of the people you worked with at Rivonia Technology. The people you select will complete a survey online. The purpose of this survey is to help us to receive feedback on how you interact with people in a variety of situations. The information will be more meaningful if you ask your former supervisor, colleagues, and the people that you supervised to complete these surveys. Make sure you choose people who know you well and who have had opportunities to work with you in a variety of situations.

"Alex, I want you also to complete a survey online, describing yourself. This will help you and me to see how your understanding of yourself matches how others see you.

> Being *versatile* means having the skills, attitudes, and competencies to productively manage the tension that naturally occurs whenever people work together.

"And now, I want to share with you an important piece of the puzzle for your success. For you to make a career change or to just change jobs in sales, you'll need to be what I call *versatile* in order to be successful. Being versatile means having the skills, attitudes, and competencies to productively manage the tension that naturally occurs whenever people work together. Not being aware of tension, focusing only on the job to be done, thinking only about the bottom line and how much profit there will be, may bring short-term results, but it won't bring you or the company success in the long run.

"I want you to do some thinking about how you feel that you relate with others. Take your time and concentrate on these three questions. Then write down your thoughts."

Smokey handed Alex a four-by-seven note card, and Alex curiously read the questions.

"Think about these questions and your responses as we continue to talk and as you visit the other members of your board. Be back here a week from Saturday at seven-thirty in the morning, and we'll talk further." Smokey got up and led Alex to the door. He asked, "Do you have any questions?"

Alex gathered up the material Smokey had given him and started for the door with a quick, "Yes, I understand and I'll start immediately. Thank you. I'll see you a week from Saturday."

Sitting in his car Alex reflected on his visit with Smokey. He thought, "Smokey certainly moves fast and to the point. It will be quite an education for me just watching him. Now, who should I give these surveys to at Rivonia? People I've worked with who know me well."

1. With whom do you work with best? Describe the situation.
2. With whom do you not like to work? Describe the situation.
3. In which work situations do you find the most satisfaction? Describe these situations.

SMOKEY'S
"Ah Ha's"

Life is the ability to adapt again.
It is not survival of the fittest,
but of the *versatile*.
—Unknown

On the Saturday morning of his appointment, Alex arrived at Smokey house at seven-thirty. He had completed his survey and all the information sheets as Smokey had requested. Contacting the people, then following up to make sure everyone had completed the survey had been time consuming, but Alex was good at getting things done.

Smokey had already downloaded Alex's profile from the computer. Alex's peers, those he had supervised and his former supervisor, had all completed a checklist of adjectives, describing Alex's behavior as the group saw it. Smokey wasn't surprised with the results.

"Alex, this information will help me to understand how others view your style of interaction. The way that others view your behavior is critical, if you want to communicate effectively, motivate, supervise, and interact with them. This information will help you to explore adjustments you might need to make in order to be successful in your new career. But first I'd like to hear your thoughts on the questions I asked you to think about."

Alex wasn't sure where to begin. He hesitantly started, "Thinking about the questions was harder than I thought it would be. I've never considered questions like these to be important."

"It's OK. We're just going to explore some new ideas that you can add to your career tool chest. Just share some of your thoughts with me," Smokey said, as he got comfortable in his favorite chair. Who did you like working with best at Rivonia? Who did you find it difficult working with? Describe the situations as you worked with each. In your work situations, what did you find the most satisfying? Describe these situations.

"Well, there are several people I like to work with. They get right down to work, don't waste time, and they make decisions quickly. There's one person I don't like to work with. He's about the exact opposite of the person I like to work with. He seems to enjoy a lot of small talk and takes forever to get to the point."

"That's good information for me to know," Smokey said, with a knowing smile. "Now, tell me about the situations that you find the most satisfying and the least satisfying.."

"Well, truthfully, I probably enjoy selling more than being a supervisor. When I was in sales, I enjoyed finding out what my customers needed and then meeting that need. I believe I'm good at taking charge of a situation and solving the problem. As a supervisor, I was frustrated when I could clearly see what needed to be done, and the salespeople couldn't solve the problem."

"Alex, let me summarize what you've just said. You enjoy situations when things move quickly, where you're in control of the situation, and where you can help others by solving their problems. You're bothered when you can't control the course of action and when others are too slow in getting things done."

Alex nodded his head and added, "Some people just don't get the results they should be getting. It seems like their minds are on other things."

"Alex, I want you to remember how you've answered my questions as you visit and observe each member of your board. It will be extremely informative to see how your answers match the answers we received in the feedback from those people with whom you've worked.

"And here's something that should interest you," Smokey said. He handed Alex a summary of the reports generated from the surveys Alex had given to the people who worked with him at Rivonia. "These reports indicate that people view you as being efficient, quick to act and to make decisions, task-oriented, able to get the job done, without getting caught up in the emotions of the job. They believe you know where you're going, that you're quick to point out to colleagues or superiors what you think."

"That pretty well hits the nail on the head," Alex said. "Doesn't everyone act and think that way?"

Smokey continued to look over Alex's summary report for a few minutes, and then responded, "Well, some of us do, Alex. I'm seen as a fast-paced, take-charge type individual."

"But," Smokey elaborated, "just because you and I prefer that style of behavior doesn't mean that we'll be effective when we're working with individuals who prefer different styles than we do. In fact, I've found that when I consistently act in a fast-paced, no-nonsense way, I'm not effective with most people.

"Discovering that everyone wasn't just like me was a real *Ah Ha*. It caught my attention!" Smokey laughed. "Some people make decisions slowly and need a lot of information. Some people rely on the relationships and the trust they have with others in order to make decisions. Some people are quick-paced, as you and I are, and they make decisions using their intuition.

"Do you remember the top line to success that Jan told you about?"

"Yes, I believe it went something like: Relationships, relationships, relationships, it is all about relationships. "

"That's pretty close, Alex," Smokey said. "How do you think the top line to success applies to what we've been talking about?"

"I have no idea how it applies to business." Alex sounded puzzled.

"Well, companies like Rivonia Technology are bought out because they aren't as productive as they need to be. Business consultants, like W. Edwards Deming and Tom Peters, realized that companies have too many managers watching over staff, attempting to control others. This type of supervision doesn't produce better products, more products, or more sales over the long-term.

"It's essential that managers help the sales and production staff to view themselves as important team members. Teams need to know that their jobs have meaning and make a difference. Staff needs to assume more responsibility for improving the quality of the product and increasing the sales.

"I've discovered that the divisions that produce the highest quality of products, with sales forces that consistently reach and exceed the sales targets, have supervisors and staff with relationships that are mutually beneficial. Relationships, relationships, relationships, all there is, are relationships.

> **Platinum Rule:**
> *Do unto others as they would have done unto themselves."*
> Joe Ratway

"So, Alex, this all means that your success as a manager, in any business, depends on your ability to understand how to develop and to maintain productive relationships with all the people with whom you come in contact in and outside your company. The success of your relationships comes down to communicating in a way that makes sense to others, not just to you. It's invaluable to always follow the Platinum Rule: *Do unto others as they would have done unto themselves."*

Alex said, "How can I possibly know what style of communication others prefer? I've always assumed that everyone prefers the same style of communication that I prefer."

"Alex, that's a normal first reaction. It seems logical to you, but people are definitely different. Understanding that people may prefer to be communicated with in different styles than you prefer is only a first step. You may have the best intentions, but people will still judge you by your actions. To be effective with others, you must communicate in a way that they can understand. It's like speaking English to a person who understands English.

"Now, I'd like to share another of my *"Ah Ha's."* It's my secret for understanding how to interact more effectively with others. This secret is what I attribute most of my success to, professionally and personally. It has helped me to understand and to make the top line to success happen.

"We act the way we do because as we grew up certain behaviors helped us to be successful in our own eyes. Over a period of time, these behaviors became habits. Habits are patterns of behavior that help us to reach important goals or help us to reduce our stress.

"Some people like a fast pace and like to be in control. Others like the pace of life to be slower, and they prefer to go with the flow. Then we have the people who prefer a logical, task-oriented, organized approach, and still there are others who are more spontaneous with their feelings and more people oriented."

Alex had a case of information overload, but he realized the importance of the information Smokey was sharing with him. He listened intently as Smokey continued. "Knowing a person's preferred behavior pattern helps me to understand what he or she values in a relationship. If I'm not aware of individual's needs and behaviors, I may see these people as being difficult, when they are, actually, just different from me."

Smokey explained that he had found an insightful model that makes sense out of all of this:

The people who focus on relationships—a slower-pace, team-players, more-asking and generally-accepting of people—prefer an Amiable style of interaction.

Those who focus on accuracy—slower-pace, controlled-emotions, detail, and a logical-presentation of information—prefer an Analytical style of interaction.

The individuals who are decisive—focused on the bottom-line, fast-paced, and want to be in charge—prefer a Driving style of interaction.

The people who appear flamboyant—high-energy, fast-paced, emoting, and in need of recognition—prefer an Expressive style of interaction.

Smokey then took a piece of paper from the desk and sketched a model to go with his explanation of the four styles of interaction.

SOCIAL STYLE MODEL™

ANALYTICAL	DRIVING
AMIABLE	EXPRESSIVE

™ SOCIAL STYLE MODEL is a Trade Mark of the TRACOM Corporation. Used with permission Copyright© 2005 by The TRACOM Corporation. Visit www.tracomcorp.com for more information.

Smokey said, "This brief explanation is an overview. We'll continue to explore these basic four different styles of behavior, as you visit with each member of your board of directors."

Alex interrupted, "When people who prefer opposite styles of interaction work together, doesn't that create problems?"

"Good question." Smokey said. "Opposites don't have to find it difficult to work together if both are willing to stretch, to listen, and to work from the other person's needs in the work relationship. This is where many of the stresses we face in life start. We tend to interpret others' actions from our own point of view. If we can learn to understand others better, we will fully be able to hear what they have to say, and we'll achieve better results as we interact with them. This, again, is that versatile behavior."

Alex looked as puzzled as he felt. "This seems as if I need to analyze what everyone is thinking. I don't know how to tell what's going through another person's mind."

Smokey clarified, "This isn't based on what is going on in the other people's minds. It's only based on the behavior you see or hear. Their behavior gives you some idea as to what style of interaction they prefer. At this point, just strictly observe their behavior. But, keep in mind, a person's behavior is only a part of his or her total personality.

> Every style of behavior can be successful in business and life when a person is able to be *versatile*.

"Another *Ah Ha* of mine is that I must be observant, and most important, I must observe others without judgment. This isn't easy to do. Remember, you must pay careful attention to what people do as well as to what they say. Their actions will tell you more than their words. Every style of behavior can be successful in business and life when a person is able to be versatile.

"Versatile behavior helps to create situations where both people come out winners.

"Alex, based on the feedback you gathered from your colleagues and supervisors at Rivonia, what style of interaction do you think they see you as preferring?" Smokey asked.

Alex felt ready to give it a try and offered, "Well, based on your description of the styles of interaction, I think people would say I use a Driving style of interaction, but I don't believe I do. I care about people and their successes, and I enjoy having fun as much as the next person, but I still have to push my salespeople to meet their sales targets."

Smokey said, "According to the feedback we received, the people at Rivonia do see you as preferring a Driving style of interaction, and it doesn't surprise me that you disagree. About seventy percent of the time, we don't view our style the same way that others do. Remember, it's not how you see yourself, but how others see you that is important. It's the impact that you have on others that is the reality you have to deal with.

"Now, as you visit with each member of your board, think of my "Ah Ha" model for interacting with others. Keep this card with you all the time and remember these two questions as you talk to and observe your different board members at work. Take notes on what you see and feel you understand."

What is her/his preferred style for interaction with others?

What behaviors do you see him/her using in order to be effective when working with others?

PUZZLING EVENTS

All my life I wanted to be somebody.
Then I realized I had to be specific.
—Lily Tomlin

At seven-thirty the next morning, Alex was at the animal hospital waiting to meet Dr. Rachel Williams. He was still confused about the purpose of observing each member of his board. To make matters worse, he was sitting beside two cats, three dogs, and their owners. He was thinking, "What a noisy place," as the dogs sniffed at his pants and occasionally barked at each other or at the cats.

Alex had never owned a pet. His kids wanted to get a dog, but they had decided to wait until summer.

Although Alex was trying to keep in mind what he and Smokey had discussed, he still felt that an animal hospital was about as far from his reality as it could get. He wondered what he could possibly learn from an animal doctor.

At that moment, Rachel burst through the door, talking a mile a minute and dispensing warmth and energy throughout the office. She greeted each person in the waiting area with a friendly good morning. Rachel took the time to pet each dog and cat and to talk with the owners about their animals, the weather, and a recent community celebration. Rachel had a bounce in her step as she moved about.

Smokey had told Alex that Rachel was very active in the community and in her church. She was currently the state veterinary association's legislative representative, and she was a single mother raising two teenage daughters, although she didn't look old enough to have teenagers. Rachel was tall and lean; she had been a runner until this past year when she developed knee problems that changed her exercise routine. Her hair was shiny black, pulled back into a tight ponytail that accentuated her long face and dark brown eyes. She was tan from hours outdoors with her dogs and her girls' soccer matches.

Watching Rachel and knowing of her involvement in so many activities made Alex wonder why she would spend so much time talking to the people in the waiting room.

Suddenly, Rachel looked over, smiled, and said, "You must be Alex. Jan Omizo told me that you'd be stopping in." She grasped Alex's hand firmly and invited him back to her office.

"I'm glad to have you here today," Rachel said. "This is a good day. There aren't too many things going on in the hospital, and we'll have some time to talk."

Alex asked, "What did Smokey and Jan tell you was the reason for my visit?"

Rachel laughed and said, "You're here to see how I work with my staff and clients. Smokey and Jan worked with me a few years ago when I was having an extremely difficult time here at the hospital. I'm always glad to share what I've learned when they ask me. But you need to know that I'm still learning, and you'll see that I still make mistakes in how I work with people. Do you have any other questions?" Then, without even pausing, Rachel said, "Let's get started."

Rachel walked quickly into the back area and greeted the technicians and the veterinary assistants. She then moved to the waiting area, where she introduced Alex to the receptionist, bookkeeper, and office manager. Each person seemed to be happy, busy, and focused on his or her job. Alex wondered if it was just a show for him.

As Rachel and Alex walked, Alex said, "I do have a few questions before we get started."

Rachel was quick to respond. "Good, what questions do you have?" But without waiting for an answer, she continued, "Let's step into examining room one and see that big dog you were sitting with in the waiting room."

Rachel made quite a fuss over the dog—particularly how beautiful he was—as she examined him. Alex had to admit the dog looked like a show dog. She asked Tad, the owner, how he was doing with his garden, and they traded stories about who had the biggest tomatoes. Without missing a beat, she turned to the assistant and asked her to find a technician to take blood samples in order to run several tests.

Alex noticed an immediate change in Tad's demeanor. He had been talking and appeared to be relaxed. Suddenly he stopped talking, moved closer to his dog, Titan, and began petting and talking to him.

Seeing a wave of concern come over Tad's face, Rachel quickly offered him a chair. She pulled another chair close to Tad and sat down. "Something I've done is bothering you, Tad?" Rachel reflected, responding to his facial expressions.

Tad looked uneasy as he replied, "Ordering blood to be drawn and those other tests must mean something. I thought this examination was to be routine. Is something wrong with Titan?"

"Oh no, I just got ahead of myself. This *is* just a routine exam. As Titan gets older, I feel it's best to check out a few things to prevent or to catch problems early. I went too fast and didn't take the time to explain what I was doing. I apologize," Rachel added in a sincere tone of voice.

Rachel then explained, in great detail, what she was checking for and why the tests were necessary. She told Tad the cost of the tests, which Alex thought was reasonable, and asked him if he had any other concerns or questions.

Tad seemed to relax, and he asked lots of questions about the examination and the blood tests. He was relieved to find that he'd get the results before he and Titan left the hospital.

Alex decided that he was glad he didn't have sales representatives like Tad. Tad had so many questions and wanted to know every detail. Alex wondered how Rachel could be so patient.

As Rachel and Alex walked out of the examining room, Rachel said, "I assumed some things in there that I shouldn't have. Often, I go too fast, and I don't consider the tension my fast pace may create. It could have been a bad situation, if I hadn't noticed Tad's concern. Now, again, what are your questions, Alex?"

Alex had to think a minute before he remembered. "What am I supposed to learn by being in an animal hospital all day?"

Rachel said, "Alex, don't you remember? I'm a member of your board of directors. Just as in a business, I can guide you in becoming more successful, although you can ignore me a lot easier than if I were on an official board of directors. Here, the choice is up to you."

Rachel added, "Always keep in mind the questions that Smokey asked you to consider. The answers will help you to gain insight that you'll need as you change careers. Watch the rest of your board members, along with me, as we interact with our clients and staff. Try to identify which actions you see that appear to build relationships beneficial to everyone."

Rachel directed the technicians as they were examining tissue samples under the microscopes and preparing other materials to be sent to an outside lab. So many things were going on at the same time that Alex wondered how Rachel kept track of everything.

Just then one of Rachel's associate veterinarians rushed through the back room with a large black dog on a gurney. The dog had been hit by a car and Alex could tell that something was drastically wrong. The dog, Mandy, was taken directly to surgery. Rachel pushed in front of the owner, Meg, who was trying to stay close to her dog.

Meg was visibly upset. She was shaking, crying, and asking to be with her dog. Rachel gently took her by the arm and led her into a private office, where she sat beside her and talked with her for about fifteen minutes. They discussed how important the dog was to Meg, and Rachel seemed very empathetic to Meg's responses. She returned to check on Meg between her appointments, always listening carefully to Meg's concerns. Finally, the doctor came out of surgery and said that Meg's dog was going to be OK. Meg and Rachel hugged each other, each one overjoyed with the news. Alex was put off by Rachel's open display of emotion, which he considered inappropriate.

Rachel's next appointment was with a family that was considering getting a pet and wanted advice from a professional. The family had only come to ask questions. The kids wanted a dog in the worst way, but the parents, Kenneth and Joan, had many concerns.

With overwhelming enthusiasm, Rachel began the meeting by sharing the joys of having a dog. Her positive feelings were just what the kids, Kennedy and Spencer, wanted to hear, but they weren't appreciated by the parents.

Joan reacted immediately. Her face flushed red and she announced that she disliked even the thought of getting a dog. She listed several specific conditions that had to be met before she would even consider it. She went on to say that she didn't appreciate Rachel getting the kids excited about a dog.

Alex noticed an immediate change in Rachel. She sat back in her chair and started listening carefully. She realized that her excitement hadn't been appropriate and was certainly not what the parents wanted to hear.

Rachel slowed down and carefully said, "I truly do want what is best for your family. What are some of your concerns about getting a dog?"

Joan was the first to respond. "I'll be the one who has to take care of it all day. I'll end up feeding and walking it. I suppose I'll be the one to pick up the droppings in the yard and the hair that sheds all over the house. I am not going to be the one responsible for a dog!"

Rachel continued to listen and asked more questions. Kenneth and Joan had well-rehearsed reasons why a dog wouldn't be a good idea for their family. Spencer and Kennedy looked pretty dejected, as if all hope of getting their very own dog was gone. Alex was happy not to be included in the conversation at all.

"Have you ever considered which dog might be best for your family?" Rachel asked. "I mean, as a family, have you actually discussed your concerns, your likes and dislikes, and then researched the different breeds to see if one would fit your needs?"

Joan, clearly frustrated, quickly replied, "No, we haven't. We've talked a lot, and we never agree."

"Well," Rachel said, "would you be interested in discussing the issues again, if I could provide some structure? If your decision is yes, we could talk about which type of dog meets your family's guidelines."

Kenneth and Joan looked at each other and Joan said. "We'd like to get this situation resolved," and Ken nodded his agreement..

"Let me suggest a couple of books that contain a series of questionnaires that will help your family to analyze your concerns and desires," Rachel said pleasantly. "This will require that you all complete the surveys and discuss your answers. If you'll take the time to work on this together, you'll come up with the answer that's right for you."

Rachel's suggestion seemed to please the whole family. They took the books, thanked Rachel, and headed home for some long conversations.

"Discussions like that, with all those questions, would drive me up a wall," Alex said. "They certainly couldn't agree on much."

"It's important that I help families make the right choices. I got carried away and almost forgot to guide them in their effort to make a decision."

"Yes," Alex said, "Joan got pretty upset when she thought you were taking the kids' side."

"That's a good observation, Alex. As I told you when we started this morning, you'll see me make mistakes in how I work with people. Joan is a very factual person. She needs to have lots of information and doesn't make decisions based on emotions. I didn't pick up on that, at first. She was frustrated and impatient with all the feelings being expressed. I realized that I needed to get the control back to her, so she could gather the amount of information she needed for her comfort level."

"What would be your guess as to whether or not they'll get the dog?" Alex asked.

"I would say they'll probably get a dog, but there will be very specific agreements made. The agreements may even need to be in writing."

"Well," Alex asked, "are all your days like this?"

"What do you mean?" Rachel said, looking puzzled.

"It's been a frantic pace all day, with things happening all over the place. It just seems chaotic to me. I'm not even sure what's going on or what I'm supposed to be learning. Your staff seems to work well together, and your clients appear to be receiving what they want and need, but where do I fit into all of this?"

Alex scratched his head and looked to Rachel for some kind of an answer.

"Well, I don't want to give you the answers. If you're going to be successful with these new skills, it will be better to discover the answers for yourself. Besides, what works for me probably won't work the same way for you. You'll discover the answers you're looking for as you reflect on the situations you observed today and as you observe the other members of your board as they interact with their staff and clients. Also carefully continue to consider the questions Smokey gave you.

"However, I will give you some coaching as to where to start. Stop for a minute and think about the various styles of interactions I was involved in today with my staff and clients. What did I do when the situation was tense or when people were anxious? We've already discussed a few of my mistakes. How did I respond to Meg when she was so upset about her dog? How did I help the family set up a plan to make a decision about getting a dog?

"Did I need to adjust my style of interaction? If so, what adjustments did I need to make in order to meet my clients' needs? Review Smokey's *"Ah Ha"* for building and maintaining relationships. Apply that information to how I interacted with my clients and staff.

"Alex," Rachel continued, "did Smokey tell you what my preferred style of interaction is? Knowing my style of interaction will help you to discover some of the answers. Besides, it's important for you to see Greg, Lonnie, and Jim before you will begin to understand some of the successful ways to interact with people."

As Alex walked away from the animal hospital, rumblings in the sky gave warning of an approaching storm.

Alex felt tired and confused. He wondered why Rachel wasn't more direct with her answers. Why didn't she just tell him what she was doing and let him decide if it was something he could use? After spending the entire day at the animal hospital, he just had more questions and felt he wasn't any better off than when he had arrived that morning.

"Rachel could be Expressive," Alex thought to himself. He tried to remember how Smokey had described the Expressive style of behavior. Rachel was certainly fast paced, exciting to be around, and she genuinely seemed to enjoy being with people. But if her style of interaction was Expressive, how was she able to slow down and pay attention to the details when she needed to? This didn't seem to be consistent with what Smokey had said about the Expressive style. Alex had no idea what he was supposed to have learned from her, and he realized that he had problems relating to Rachel's style.

He did know one thing. He was frustrated, confused and more impatient than ever with this painstaking process.

ARE PEOPLE REALLY THIS WAY

We buy our freedom
by our results.
—Author Unknown

It was nearly seven in the morning when Greg Drydon, the school principal, greeted Alex at the entrance of Jefferson Middle School. Greg had a magnificent smile, sky-blue eyes, and blond unruly hair. He appeared to be in his early forties. He had broad shoulders, a spiffy appearance, and he seemed to be very much at ease. Greg acted as if he'd known Alex for years.

"Hey, Alex," Greg said, as he firmly shook Alex's hand. "I'm sorry we can't talk right now, but I need to meet with a student who's experiencing discipline problems in his classes. He's been quite a challenge for the teachers this year. It's hard to keep him in school, and when he's here, he intimidates the other students.

"The student, Mike, his parents, the counselor, and his five teachers will be in the meeting. I've asked his parents for permission for you to sit in on the conference, and they've agreed. Please come into the conference room and meet the others."

After the round of introductions, Alex settled into his chair and decided this conference wouldn't be hard to conduct. All Greg needed to do was to tell the student and his parents what behavior would be accepted in school. Alex thought the conference should take about ten minutes, tops.

Greg started the meeting by sharing the latest episode. Mike had transferred to the school three months earlier and was intimidating other students into giving him their lunch money. Some students had given him money, and others had refused. The students who hadn't given Mike their money ended up in a pushing and shoving match with him. Two other students were also being disciplined for their involvement in the disturbances.

Out of the fifty-five days that Mike was supposed to be in school, he had attended only forty days. Greg had asked the teachers to review Mike's class behavior. Each teacher had a slightly different problem with Mike, but the solution seemed obvious to Alex. Mike had done no homework, nor had he worked in class when time was provided. He disturbed other students in and between classes. The school couldn't accept this type of behavior.

Mike and his parents, John and Molly, were asked to comment on the problems that had been presented. Mike mumbled something that Alex couldn't hear and then he was silent. Molly was the first to speak up. "Mike had no problems at his other school. I have to wonder what's going on here. Is this just a big deal about nothing?"

At this point, Mike stood up and held on tightly to the edge of the table. He looked directly at his parents and said, "I never wanted to move. I don't like this school!" He pursed his lips. "The kids are snobs; they're weird, not my type. I don't fit in. I missed school because I was sick."

As the meeting continued, everyone appeared to be thoughtfully listening to Mike's concerns and to those of his parents. John made it known that he didn't believe Mike would intimidate or take money from other students. What puzzled Alex the most was that it seemed as if Greg was agreeing with Mike and his parents. Greg allowed the conference to go on and on.

As the conference slowly moved forward, Alex paid close attention. He noticed that Greg had changed his posture and his expression, as if something had happened within him. He expressed how much he and the staff cared about Mike and stated that they wanted him to do well in school. Greg explained some of the school programs that were available to help Mike talk about his anger and his displeasure with Jefferson Middle School and the students. Greg then took a firm stand on the behavior he expected from Mike in the classroom, at lunch, and anywhere on the school grounds. He made it clear that he wouldn't accept anything less.

The conference took almost an hour. When it was finished, everyone had agreed on a plan as to what Mike was going to do to change his behavior and what the school and his parents would do to support him. Alex felt that Mike wasn't wholeheartedly accepting the agreement, but at least he said he'd give it a try. After such a rough start, Alex was surprised to see that everyone left smiling, shaking hands, and appearing to feel satisfied with the outcome.

Keeping up with Greg as they walked wasn't nearly as hard as it had been with Rachel. Greg went directly from the conference to meet the kids as they arrived on the school buses. He seemed to know most of their names, and it was obvious they knew him. Seeing the students file into the school brought back a flood of memories for Alex about his own junior high school experiences. Sadly, his memories of his school days weren't all that great.

As they walked back into the school, Greg explained, "The conference went longer than I thought it would. I didn't mean for that to happen. I believe the parents were beginning to believe that I was agreeing with them."

"I thought you were agreeing with the parents, too," Alex shrugged.

"That's a problem I sometimes get myself into. When emotions get high, I appear to be agreeing and going along. I caught myself in that situation during the conference, and I had to very purposefully clarify what I know is best for Mike and the school."

Greg admitted, "Pushing hard for a positive agreement is difficult for me when a lot of emotion is present. It's something I have to work consistently to improve, if I want to be a more effective, successful leader."

Alex found Greg's comment to be very interesting. Greg had planned for the conference, yet he still had to adjust as the conference moved ahead. Alex wondered if Greg should have planned better, or if it was just as important to make adjustments when needed.

After school started, Greg had conferences scheduled with two of his science teachers to review their yearly goals. He told the teachers, Mindy and Dennis, the time of day that he planned to visit their classrooms in order to observe them in a teaching situation. He asked each teacher to explain briefly the objective of the lesson that he would be observing.

Within the hour, Alex and Greg were sitting in the back of Mindy's classroom, watching as she presented the lesson material and handed out questions the students were to answer.

Mindy circulated and worked with small discussion groups, encouraging them to think about the experiments and the results. The students were applying what they were learning to projects, which seemed pretty interesting to Alex. The classroom looked more like a business or work setting. The students were first given a problem to work on. They then developed strategies for solving the problem through their research, using a variety of resources from inside and outside the classroom.

At the end of the class, Greg met with Mindy to review his observations. Greg encouraged Mindy to critique herself. He clarified her comments and gave her concrete examples of the good teaching strategies she had used at several specific times. The conference was very supportive of Mindy's teaching qualities, yet Alex was surprised to hear that Mindy had specific suggestions for what she could do to improve. In Alex's estimation she was an excellent teacher. She was open to ideas and wanted to learn new and better ways to help students. Alex's experiences in meetings with his salespeople sure hadn't been like this.

Alex was amazed at the open interaction between Greg and Mindy. They both seemed relaxed and earnest as they shared ideas for ways to improve. He wished that the people he had managed had been as open and honest about their performances. Profits would have increased and he would have had one terrific sales force! He wondered if Greg's success was a result of the way that Greg worked with his staff, or if Greg just had better people.

After the conference, Greg talked to the students and staff members as he walked through the halls toward the lunchroom to see how things were going.

During lunch, he wandered through the tables, talking to everyone. Greg knew the students' first names and joked with them in a carefree, open manner. The kids seemed genuinely to like Greg. One student stopped him to tell a joke. Another student told him about a recital she would be in on Sunday and said she hoped he would attend.

This was a much different school atmosphere from the one Alex remembered. Alex and his friends hadn't liked their principal, and the principal had never joked and talked with them as Greg did. There was a different atmosphere at Jefferson Middle School. Alex didn't know just how to describe it at this point.

There was no time to sit around or to relax. Greg completed his teacher evaluation with Dennis and then sat in on an unexpected parent-teacher conference at the teacher's request. Greg's day seemed constantly to involve a high degree of interaction with and for others.

Fifteen minutes after the dismissal bell, there was a meeting in the library for all teachers and support staff.

Greg began the meeting by recognizing specific achievements of some staff members. He thanked the teachers who helped to chaperone a school dance. Two teachers were recognized for obtaining one-thousand-dollar grants for each of their classrooms. A custodian was nominated by the staff and presented a district plaque for outstanding service.

The staff meeting continued in an informal manner. Greg had written the agenda on a flip chart and each item was discussed. The staff seemed to have a great deal of input into how the school was operating.

Greg announced that it was time to establish the new hall-, lunch-, and bus-duty schedules for the next year. He wanted the staff to decide how the schedules were to be developed. Several staff members wanted Greg to develop the schedules and just hand them out. Others, who felt that staff needed to take that responsibility, volunteered to be on the task force to draw up a recommendation to be presented to the total staff at the next meeting for approval. Greg helped them with guidelines for the needed coverage and moved on to the next item, report cards.

The teachers introduced a recommendation that they had been researching on the use of letter grades on report cards. Their research clearly supported the idea that this type of report card was not effective. The teachers wanted to replace the current report card with a new card that would indicate student progress toward meeting the standards in each course.

Greg listened carefully, but he appeared to be uncomfortable with the recommendation. He considered the request for a minute and then introduced some questions: "What will the students say about this change? Did the parents have input into this proposal? How will we inform the parents and students of this new reporting process?"

Without raising an objection, Greg was able to point out successfully that the teachers needed to check with other resources before making any recommendations. He gave them positive feedback for their hard work, stated his support of the concept, and helped them with ideas to move ahead.

The staff meeting continued in this fashion until most of the agenda had been covered. Greg asked if the rest of the items could wait until the next meeting. It was late and the staff immediately agreed. Many stayed to talk for the next fifteen to twenty minutes.

Greg walked over to Alex and said, "Well, that does it for the day, but I have a PTA executive board meeting at seven this evening. Would you like to attend?"

Alex was quick to respond, "Yes, I'd like to, but I need to get home." The truth was that he was worn out. The pace with Greg hadn't been as fast as with Rachel, but the constant contact with people and the continuous effort required to find acceptable resolutions had taken a toll on Alex. And he was merely an observer!

"Well, Alex," Greg followed up, "do you have any thoughts about the day and what happened?"

"The day wasn't at all what I expected," Alex answered. "I thought you'd just tell your staff what to do, without asking for their input. If you had, I think things would have been completed faster and more efficiently. And if you had been more direct with Mike and his parents this morning, you could have saved a great deal of time. As for the teachers that you observed, you could have just told them what teaching style you'll accept. The staff meeting was okay, but there again, a lot of time was taken up by input and discussions. You're the leader. They expect you to tell them what to do, don't they?"

"Alex, you make some good points. I might have been more efficient if I had done as you suggest. But would I have been as effective? As a member of your board, I want to give you a few questions to consider." Greg leaned back, thought for a minute, and then stated his questions.

"Were the differences in opinions, recognized, and built upon in order to arrive at even better decisions?"

"Is it important to alter your approach when you realize you're not communicating what you want to be communicating?"

"Were the decisions, following the group discussions, effective decisions?"

"As a manager, do you want your staff to openly give you their best thoughts and ideas? If so, how can you make sure they feel free to give you their best thinking?"

"Do you want your staff to feel that they are supported and important and that they are a significant part of the team?"

"Think about these questions before you answer. Discuss them with Smokey for his thoughts. To me, being a leader or a manager means that I need to be aware of the tension others experience in each interaction. It's my responsibility to help create situations where better decisions can be made and people are able to be more interdependent. A leader can't be everywhere and have all the information required to make the best decisions."

Alex interrupted, "You asked me for my thoughts about the day. Help me to understand what you were thinking during the meetings and interactions."

> "It's my belief that the best decisions are made when the people involved feel that they can be open and not afraid to make mistakes.

"Alex, that's a fair question," Greg said. "It's my belief that the best decisions are made when the people involved feel that they can be open and not afraid to make mistakes. The decisions made in order to help Mike were the result of input from many teachers, along with Mike and his parents. The teacher evaluations were successful because the teachers felt secure enough to critique themselves, to discuss ideas with me, and to come up with their own suggestions for self improvement. My role is to keep the focus on what is best for students in all decision making and to help others learn to take responsibility for solutions."

Alex, once again, walked away from his visit overwhelmed with more questions, more information, and more confusion.

Alex thought that Rachel and Greg definitely had two very different styles of interaction. Both really liked to be with people; both were friendly. But Rachel was faster paced and seemed to be more scattered in her approach. Greg was slower in his interactions; he didn't have to be in the center of things, yet others seemed to respect and to listen to him. Alex wondered if Greg was an Amiable, or maybe, an Analytical in his style of interaction.

As he reviewed the day, Alex continued to think about Greg. His style of interaction could be Amiable. He liked people; he worked to build agreements and teams. Yet when faced with difficult situations, he pushed for decisions. How did all this fit? Was his style Amiable? "What," Alex thought, "am I not under-standing?"

And how did these pieces of the puzzle fit into Smokey's *"Ah Ha's"* for under-standing one's working style and with Relationships, relationships, relationships, that is all there is are relationships?

SOME THINGS ARE BEGINNING TO ADD UP

Be the change you are trying to create.
—Gandhi

The next day Alex telephoned Smokey. Smokey sensed the high degree of emotion in Alex's voice. Alex said, "I need to see you for just a few minutes. This whole experience with my board of directors is amazing and at the same time upsetting. Having had the opportunity to observe people working with their staff and clients has me really thinking. May I come over in the morning?"

Smokey was anxious to hear what Alex had discovered. "Sure, be here at seven-thirty and I'll fix breakfast."

Although it was Saturday morning, Alex was up early and on his way to see Smokey. He and Linda had talked until late Friday night, putting thoughts together, so Alex could clearly communicate his ideas and questions to Smokey. Linda had been helpful in listening and helping to clarify the interactions Alex had observed over the past few days. She had always understood people better than Alex. With her help, he worked hard to understand and to summarize his experiences, but Alex still felt a disturbing confusion about his visits with Rachel and Greg.

Alex thought about the questions Smokey had given him. What were the interaction styles of Rachel and Greg? If he were their supervisor, what would he need to do in order to work effectively with each one individually?

As he drove, Alex considered his experiences with his board members, attempting to understand their way of working. Rachel was fast-paced and emotional and looked at the big picture. Her preferred style of interaction was probably Expressive.

Greg took care of people, listened, and was extremely patient; his style of interaction was probably Amiable.

Now what would help Alex to work with each one effectively?

The biggest piece to the puzzle, Alex decided, was that they were both effective, yet so different. How could this information help him to be more effective? This wasn't an easy process and he still doubted that it had any validity, but he hoped talking with Smokey would help.

Before Alex had even taken his place at the breakfast table, he started telling Smokey about his visits with Rachel and Greg.

"I'm physically worn out following them around. I've tried hard to learn and to understand how they effectively work with people. After all this time and energy, I've seen so much, yet I'm not sure what I've learned. I have lots of questions; that's why I needed to see you this morning."

"I could tell over the telephone that you're pretty confused, and yet I would say excited about your adventures. Start by telling me about your visits with Rachel and Greg," Smokey said.

"I don't get it. Why are Rachel and Greg so caring and concerned about the people they work with?" Alex started. "Their first priority sure doesn't seem to be profits or results. Business, to me, means getting things done. Results and profits are the bottom line, not spending a lot of time chitchatting."

"You and I think alike, Alex. Do you remember what I told you that I believe is the top line to success?"

"You said, 'Relationships, relationships, relationships, that is all there is: are relationships.' But I don't know how relationships get things done, get results, or get to the bottom line, profit." Alex shook his head slowly.

"Did Rachel and Greg get things done?" Smokey asked, already knowing what the answer would be.

Alex took a minute and said, "Yes, as I think about it. They accomplished many things. I was surprised by what they were able to get done.

"Rachel was in a hurry and requested that lab tests be run, before she had explained to the dog's owner what she was doing. The owner was quite upset, but it turned out okay. Rachael noticed his distress, talked to him, gave him the information he needed, and answered his questions. He left content and pleased with Rachael.

"Greg had a nasty situation with a young boy who was creating problems in school; his parents were supporting his actions. Greg made it clear what behavior he and the school expected, but he also spent time understanding and listening to the parents and the boy. When the conference was over, the parents, the boy, the teachers, and Greg had developed a plan that each liked and supported.

"But why do they spend so much time with each person? Their staffs get paid to get the work done. If they'd just do their jobs, there wouldn't be a need for all this unnecessary talking. Greg and Rachel spend a lot of time trying to understand their clients and to get input from their staffs before any decisions are made or actions taken. Most of the time they go with their staffs' decisions anyway. I'm sure that Greg and Rachel already know what the best decision is going to be. They'd save a lot of time if they just told their staffs what to do."

Smokey summarized what he heard Alex say, "You believe Rachel and Greg get good results and leave their staff and customers feeling positive about their interactions. However, you feel they take an unrealistic amount of time interacting with their staff."

"Absolutely," Alex agreed.

Smokey quickly continued before Alex could add anything. "You're bothered by the amount of time Greg and Rachel spend with their staffs and clients on a personal basis in order to build relationships. You believe this can't be justified in a business concerned about the bottom line."

"Yes, that's what I see," Alex replied.

> Have you ever thought that we might create tension by assuming that our expectations are obvious, understood, and shared by other people?

"Alex, have you ever thought that we might create tension by assuming that our expectations are obvious, understood, and shared by other people?" Smokey asked. "And if the tension between us gets too high, it hurts the results or the bottom line?"

"I'm very clear when I state my expectations for my sales staff and there are few, if any, questions when I get through," Alex said proudly.

"You may remember I told you that versatility is my biggest *Ah Ha* for interacting effectively with others," Smokey said. "Versatility means effectively handling the tension that is normal in much of the interaction we have with people. Tension, itself, isn't bad; it's natural. It's only harmful if it gets too high, stays around too long, and isn't dealt with in a constructive way by either person.

"So, when you feel that you're being clear as you state your expectations to your sales staff, and they don't ask questions, it could mean they understand, but it may also mean there is too much tension for them to respond. They may feel it won't do any good, or they may be too threatened to ask questions. Your staff may have learned it's better to be silent, not to cause more tension, because of the way you respond if they ask questions."

Alex was surprised and quickly defended himself: "I have an open door policy. My staff knows they can talk to me anytime that they have a problem. I encourage them to ask questions. A good debate makes for good thinking."

"Having an open door policy and having staff members who feel they can be open are two entirely different things," Smokey stated. "Alex, when a person feels threatened or feels a high degree of tension in a relationship, he or she will not usually take the risk to be open, to ask questions, or to offer ideas, especially with a supervisor.

"Think about the staffs that you've just observed. You said they're productive and seem to like their jobs. What do you think motivates them? Why are Rachel and Greg so successful with their staffs and their clients? Do their staffs have an important say in decision making?"

Smokey had fixed a marvelous breakfast, and he suggested they eat and continue the questions later.

Alex ate slowly and talked to Smokey about his hobbies. He found that they both enjoyed fishing, but neither went often. Alex asked Smokey about his family, and he was proud to tell Smokey about Linda, Stephanie, and Mitch. They also spent time in silence, which Alex used to gather his thoughts.

The short break was a welcome reprieve from what Alex had considered a tense situation; he hadn't been sure how to respond to Smokey's questions. Smokey's comments had certainly caused him think.

Alex's mind was filled with questions. Were there better ways to be more productive than he had been in the past? Were there more effective ways to work with people than he had used? Didn't other people speak out about what they thought? Didn't other people want results first? Weren't all people like him and want to be treated the same way that he wanted to be treated? Did the members of his sales staff feel that they could offer suggestions and share their thoughts?

Alex finished his last bite and Smokey took their plates to the sink and asked, "Well, what have you thought about the questions I've asked? What do you think motivates the staffs you observed? What makes Rachael and Greg so successful with their staffs and their customers?"

> When relationships are meaningful for both people, the results will be more effective and positive.

"Well," Alex started slowly, "maybe I learned more from Rachel and Greg than I realized. If I'm beginning to understand your "*Ah Ha's*" for interaction and versatility, you feel that Rachel and Greg are actively aware that others like to be treated in their own preferred style. If they see that the tension in the relationship is going up, they act appropriately to try to reduce that tension to a productive level. When relationships are meaningful for both people, the results will be more effective and positive."

"That's a great start, Alex," Smokey said, with a sense of accomplishment.

Alex shrugged and paused reflectively, then he said, "I can see how this interaction system might work, but I'm not clear enough to come up with ready answers. Actually, I'm not sure I believe all of it."

Smokey acknowledged Alex's comment by saying, "I don't expect you to accept this "*Ah Ha*" of mine unless it fits for you and the people you'll be working with in your new career."

That snapped Alex back to reality. He nervously thought, "I need to find a job and is any of this stuff going to help me?"

Smokey and Alex concluded their conversation, and Alex left to prepare for his visits with Jim Watson and Lonnie Phillips

Back at home, Alex sat quietly trying to recall his discussions with Smokey. He remembered the tension he felt when Smokey asked for answers to his questions. Alex hadn't been sure what to say. He had appreciated that Smokey backed off and allowed him time to think; he was then able to respond thoughtfully.

Alex raised his index finger in an *"Ah Ha"* gesture, tapped his forehead and chuckled. Alex thought, "Smokey is amazing! He listens carefully and then summarizes to make sure he understood what I've said. He keeps just the right amount of pressure on, so I'm able to answer, yet not become upset. I wonder if I caused a lot of tension and anxiousness with my sales staff at Rivonia."

"I'm going to pay extremely close attention to Jim Watson and Lonnie Phillips to see what they do in difficult situations," Alex thought, as he dozed off into a peaceful Saturday afternoon nap.

TREAT THEM
AS THEY WANT
TO BE TREATED

Versatility is the ability
to be present,
to understand the interaction,
and adjust to make the relationship
mutually productive
—Gerald L. Prince

Jim Watson's The Way We Were, an antiques and collectibles shop, didn't open until ten each morning, so Alex took time to think through the upcoming visit. He reflected on his conversations with Smokey, the visits with Rachel and Greg, and the questions he needed to answer about each member of his board.

Alex arrived twenty minutes early, parked in front of Jim's shop, and waited impatiently for the day to begin. Jim arrived at ten on the dot, parked his car on the side street, and walked directly to the front door. He greeted Alex with a fast smile. Jim was a tall, lean man who appeared to be in his mid-fifties, with striking blue eyes and salt-and-pepper hair. He was wearing a Gatsby-style shirt, blue striped with no collar, and a pair of obviously well tailored khaki slacks. Alex thought he looked as if he'd just walked out of *The J. Peterman Company Catalog*. Jim walked quickly and had perfect posture. Alex wondered if he could have had a military background.

Alex met Jim at the door and in a low voice introduced himself. After a brief exchange, Jim went about the business of opening his shop for the day. He quickly looked around the store and noticed that a small side window was open. He turned to Alex and said in a direct calm voice, "Alex, please don't touch anything. Someone has broken into my shop. Go next door to the barber shop and call the police, while I see what's been taken."

Alex quickly left the shop and went next door, where he introduced himself to the barber and asked him to telephone the police. "Tell them that The Way We Were, the shop next door, has been burglarized." As Alex returned to the shop, he considered the structured step-by-step routine Jim had used to open his shop. Alex was curious how Jim could be so cool and methodical given the seriousness of the situation. Alex knew that if he had been in Jim's shoes, he would have been furious!

Needless to say, the next few hours were nothing like Alex had planned. There were policemen in and around the building, dusting for fingerprints, looking for stolen merchandise, and possible clues. This event did provide Alex with an excellent chance to observe Jim as he talked with the policemen and checked his store to determine exactly what had been taken.

Jim met the policemen at the front door and introduced himself. The policeman who seemed to be in charge asked Jim to start from the beginning, to tell him in as much detail as possible as to what had happened.

Jim thoughtfully began, "I arrived at precisely ten this morning. As I entered the front door, I noticed the window on the north side was up a little. As I got closer to the window, I saw that it had been pried open and the wood was broken in the left hand corner. I immediately checked the shelves on the wall where my collection of Tiffany lamps is displayed and discovered three of the lamps were gone: A twelve-light lily Tiffany Favrile glass and bronze table lamp, a Tiffany turtle-back tile and bronze desk lamp and a Tiffany curtain border leaded glass and bronze floor lamp. All three are authentic, numbered lamps, with the original bases and shades, signed by L.C. Tiffany.

Jim said in a calm and exacting manner, "I then turned to Alex, the gentleman over there, and asked him to go next door to the barber shop and call the police."

Jim handed the policeman pictures of the three lamps and continued, "You'll find a detailed description of each lamp on the back of the picture. I keep photos of all my more valuable items.

"After asking Alex to make the phone call, I checked the rest of my shop. Nothing else seems to have been disturbed. However, it will take me some time to make sure the lamps are the only items taken. The thieves seemed to know exactly what they wanted and took only the Tiffany lamps."

"I suppose you're wondering who Alex is," Jim said to the policeman. Without pausing, he continued, "He's a business associate who is here to talk with me about how I run my business and work with clients."

"Great," Alex thought impatiently, "now I'll be a suspect and have to answer a lot of questions."

The policeman did have a few questions for Alex. He seemed most interested in why Alex was there, what his interest was in antiques, and what he hoped to learn from Jim Watson.

Alex hesitantly offered, "The first time I met Jim was at ten this morning. We met in front of the shop, just before Jim discovered the burglary. Jim was referred to me as a person who can help me to better understand relationships and working with clients."

At that point, Alex decided he had better stop without mentioning his career change and his board of directors. He decided the policeman might not believe anything he had to say.

As Alex stood to the side of the shop watching Jim talk and work, he realized he was learning some things. He could see that the way Jim interacted with the police officers changed as he talked in a different manner with each officer. Alex had no idea why Jim changed his approach from one officer to the other.

After another hour, the officers had completed their investigation at the shop. The policeman who had talked with Jim the most said, "I wish everyone would be as thorough as you are. My job would be a lot easier, more stolen merchandise would be recovered, and thieves would be apprehended. You've kept detailed records with precise descriptions. That's all for now, but I'll get back to you when we have any additional information. If you think of anything, please call me."

Jim added quickly, "I have an associate who, right now, is providing the large antiques malls, private dealers, auction houses, and shop owners in the area with descriptions of the lamps, along with the pictures. With this information, they'll be informed enough to be on the lookout for the stolen lamps. Maybe the thief will try to sell them quickly. I'll notify the antiques trade papers covering each state and provide them with photos and necessary information. I also intend to offer a reward."

"Good idea," the policeman said, as he headed out the door.

Alex was quite pleased with himself for the observations he had made during the discussions between Jim and the policemen. He felt he had been aware of some good communication between them. Now Alex decided that he would take a risk to see if he truly did understand.

"Jim, what a terrible shock for you to find your valuable lamps missing!" Alex said.

"You don't know the half of it. The lamps are valuable, but the lily Favrile lamp has sentimental value. You see, it's the first lamp my wife bought when we decided to open our own business. We never intended to sell it. It has sort of been our store mascot. Thank you for your concern, Alex," Jim responded.

Flushed with one success, Alex decided to try his newfound skills again. "The policeman was astonished to receive so much information from you about your shop and the lamps."

"Well, Alex, I knew from his questions that he wanted a lot of details; those details will help him do his job to find my lamps. I gave him all the information I had. Acquiring the history, the details, and the information about antiques is the part of this job that excites me the most. I have a library filled with books, plus there are numerous sites on the Internet that I use to research the antiques I buy," Jim said.

"Well, it sure pleased him! When the policeman was talking with me, he said he wished everyone could be as observant and keep track of things the way you do," Alex said with enthusiasm.

Within a few minutes, a young couple came into the store and started browsing. Alex discovered, from overhearing their conversations, that they were recently married; their names were Mark and Kami. They picked up a few pieces of small furniture and looked them over carefully. Then Kami stopped by the jewelry cases. She looked absolutely fascinated, her eyes drawn to the antique brooches.

Jim approached the couple and started a conversation, "You have good taste in jewelry. The pieces in this case are from my wife's private collection. She recently decided to part with them; each is rare, unique, one of a kind. Could I show you a few of them?"

Kami said, "Yes! I'd love to see them all!"

Jim brought out the center jewelry pad that displayed about a dozen exquisite Victorian brooches. He carefully placed each brooch on a soft black cloth on the jewelry case counter top.

The couple looked at several brooches. Kami instantly focused on one extraordinary piece, hand carved from a single piece of coral, containing multiple flowing colors. Her eyes sparkled as she held the brooch in her hand.

Alex, being a salesman, could feel a sale about to be made as he watched Kami's reaction. He was interested to see how Jim would close the sale.

Jim smiled as he watched Kami. "Good choice. That cameo brooch was hand carved in 1873. It's a signed piece and is coral, not shell. Notice the intricate detail of the hand-carving. It's rare to find a piece with such extraordinary carving of the face, blouse, and hair. You can even see a small brooch carved on the figure's blouse. I've researched the artist and discovered some fascinating information. Would you like to read what I've come up with?"

"No, not right now." Kami put the brooch down suddenly and then moved back to the furniture.

Jim stood behind the counter with a bewildered look on his face. He put some of the brooches away, but left the one that Kami was interested in alone on the black cloth. It stood out and looked beautiful, distinctively displayed against the black background.

Within a few minutes, Kami returned to the jewelry case to look at the brooch again. She turned it over and over, looking at it closely and from a distance.

Jim cautiously asked, "Do you have any questions about the brooch?"

"Do you think it would look good on me?" she sincerely asked.

"Well, let's check it out. Put it on your jacket, so you can see how it will look. Right over there is a full-length mirror where you can see it clearly."

The brooch was truly smashing on her. Mark said he loved it, too, and wanted to buy it for her.

That was enough for Kami. With a bit of hesitation, yet with direct-eye contact, Kami asked, "How much is it?"

"We've priced it, I believe modestly, at $350.00."

The couple's faces glowed with excitement over their new purchase. As Jim was processing the credit card, he asked again, "Is there any information that you'd like to know about the brooch?"

"No," Kami firmly responded, "I love it, and that's enough for me!"

After the couple left the shop, Alex turned to Jim and asked, "What just happened there? They bought an expensive piece of jewelry and didn't want to know the artist's name or anything about it?"

Jim had a big smile on his face and laughed, "Alex, I almost talked myself out of a sale. It was *my* need to give them all the information about the brooch, because I love the history. Kami was excited about the way it looked on her. She had already sold herself. I tried to give her information that she didn't want or need. It frustrated her, and she had to get away from me for a few minutes.

> I forgot to consider the style interaction model and how my style can be effective or ineffective as I communicate with others.

"Alex, you see, I'm the one who likes to know everything there is to know about my antiques. My need for detail and information isn't everyone else's need. When I saw her back away, I knew I had done it again. She wanted the brooch because it was extraordinary. She didn't want or need to know all the information and details that are so important to me."

"Wow, you really were observant! How did you know to back off and give her some time?" Alex questioned.

"Well, that's the *"Ah Ha"* for interacting with people that Smokey told you about. I forgot to consider the style interaction model and how my style can be effective or ineffective as I communicate with others. When I remembered the model, things made sense to me.

"As you probably can guess, my style of interaction is described as Analytical. With the policeman, I was in my element. He wanted as much detail as possible about the items that were taken from my shop. I was comfortable giving him detailed descriptions of the lamps and information about how I noticed the shop had been burglarized. I communicated effectively with the officer, and, as you said, he left saying he wished everyone were as observant and organized as I am."

"Why didn't your Analytical interaction style approach work as well with Kami and Mark?"

"I got carried away with my own excitement about the brooch. It's such a unique and rare piece! I wanted her to know everything I know about it, famous artist, along with outstanding quality. Face it, I was trying to give Kami more information than she wanted or needed. Her need for the brooch was because she loved it and the way it looked on her. My need was for her to appreciate its excellent history and the detailed craftsmanship," Jim said, laughing at himself.

"I don't know if I'll ever get the hang of this. Do I have to change with each person I meet?" Alex asked with a frown.

"The answer is that you have to know yourself and to be aware not to treat others as *you* want to be treated. The secret is to treat them as they want to be treated," Jim replied.

"A major part of this "*Ah Ha*" is to keep in mind that everyone doesn't communicate in the same way. I had to adjust my thinking; it's like speaking a foreign language to a person who doesn't understand the language. If I want to communicate clearly, I need to speak a language the person can understand. I needed to make the adjustment in order to sell the brooch."

Jim's eyes were serious with the importance of what he was saying. "It's like Smokey says, the top line to success is Relationships, relationships, relationships, that is all there is, are relationships. If I take care of the top line and carry quality products, the bottom line, profit, will take care of itself."

Experiencing information overload, Alex slowly left Jim's shop and started home.

He decided to drive to a small park where he used to play as a boy. Alex sat quietly on a bench and reflected on his day. He needed to try to untangle all that had happened at Jim's shop.

"Jim most likely has an Analytical interaction style," Alex thought. "He's quite amazing in his ability to understand different styles of behavior and to make split-second adjustments when he's communicating with people."

Alex continued to mull over the day, and he did feel a touch of success. He had been able to make some accurate observations of behaviors, and he had recognized the adjustments that Jim made.

Having observed Rachel, Greg, and Jim as they interacted with their clients caused Alex to do some critical thinking. Did he drive customers and the people he supervised away by not recognizing the best way to communicate with them? He did focus on getting the job done, but did he force his preferred style of communication onto others? Was he sensitive to others' feelings? Were feelings important in communicating? How did he come across to others? Would developing stronger relationships really contribute to the bottom line? How could he learn to adapt his style of interaction with others, in midstream, as Rachel and Greg did?

BALANCING PEOPLE AND RESULTS

If we don't understand
behavior, we believe it
is wrong.
—Author unknown

Alex was up early to meet Lonnie Phillips, a local attorney well known in the community for her negotiation skills. As he entered the elevator, Alex reviewed his agenda. He planned to observe Lonnie closely as she worked with colleagues and her staff, especially when they were tense, angry, silent, or talking too much. This visit could be exciting; Lonnie had been featured in newspaper articles several times for her ability to negotiate successfully difficult situations in the community.

Alex was glad he was observing Lonnie last, after he had a chance to watch the others and to talk with Smokey. He was beginning to realize that he might not have communicated effectively with his staff at Rivonia.

Accepting the idea that he needed to make changes in the way that he interacted with others was a good start. It was still important to get bottom-line results. But it was also important to listen to others, let them know that their ideas are important, and that they are important, too. He hoped that by talking with and observing Lonnie he could become aware of how to handle difficult situations. This would help him to be seen as a strong person with skills as a better communicator. In Alex's mind, the worst possible image was to be seen as soft or wimpy.

As Alex entered Lonnie's office, he could see a great deal of activity. Lonnie was meeting with her assistant and motioned for Alex to come into her office and take a seat.

Her office was well decorated with pictures of her family and pets and with mementoes that had been gathered on vacations and from places she had visited. The office had an informal feeling, yet seemed businesslike. Everything was in its place and appeared to have a purpose.

Lonnie stood and greeted him, "You must be Alex. Smokey described you perfectly! I'm glad to meet you. Please sit here while I review the day with my assistant."

As Lonnie worked with Barbara, her assistant, Alex carefully watched her. Lonnie was a tall African American woman, brimming with confidence and looking the part of a successful attorney. She wore an understated elegantly tailored black suit over a white linen blouse, topped off by a stunning gold brooch on the collar and earrings to match. Her instructions to Barbara were precise and detailed.

However, after they finished with business, Lonnie asked Barbara how her grandchild, Atticus, had done in his school play and if he liked his new teacher.

Alex learned that Barbara's grandchild was named for Atticus Finch, a lawyer in the novel *To Kill a Mockingbird*, who was known for his strong sense of morality and fair play. Alex couldn't remember if he had read the book, but he recalled that the character in the movie version had been played by Gregory Peck. Barbara told Alex that her grandchild's full name was Atticus Jacob. Alex thought, "I bet his friends call him A.J."

Following Lonnie's quick pace, Alex sat in the chair she pointed toward and said, "It's a pleasure meeting you. I appreciate the chance to watch and learn from you."

"I once worked with a board of directors as you're doing now. In fact, I still meet occasionally with my board. Smokey and Jan are important members of it. There's so much to learn, and they are masters at coaching me to be more effective in how I interact with people."

Alex said, "It's hard for me to believe you need coaching. From everything I hear and read, you're one of the best communicators and make a pretty good living negotiating with groups and individuals."

> I have to work constantly in order to be aware of what people are thinking and feeling if I want to continue achieving successful agreements.

"Well, thank you for the compliment on my skills and my financial success. I have to work constantly in order to be aware of what people are thinking and feeling if I want to continue achieving successful agreements. I focus intensely in order to get things accomplished, and I usually know exactly how to proceed with the task. However, sometimes, when I think I know what others are thinking and feeling, I tend to move toward solutions or answers before I give them an opportunity to think or to express themselves. Jan has helped me by getting me to slow down, listen, and pay closer attention to what people aren't saying, too."

"What do you mean by what people aren't saying?" Alex questioned.

"Well, it seems only about seven percent of a message is contained in the words people speak; the rest of the message is nonverbal," Lonnie answered.

"I have no idea what you mean by a nonverbal message. Don't people say what they want and what they mean?" Alex asked in a confused tone.

"Does it upset you that you will need to be able to understand more than just the words people say?" Lonnie asked.

"Exactly! It's ridiculous if people can't plainly say what they want," Alex huffed.

"Alex, you see yourself as an up-front guy, and you expect others to be just like you," Lonnie clarified.

"Whoa, that's just what Smokey is trying to teach me! Everyone isn't just like me and I need to understand that. As Smokey would say, that's an '*Ah Ha*'!" Alex laughed as he settled back in his chair to relax.

"You're right. It is hard to realize that others think differently than we do. That's the reason it's extremely important to look for the nonverbal messages, body movements, use of hands, facial expressions, tone of voice, pace of speech, and other behaviors. This concept is essential as we try to understand others.

"When I'm trying to understand the frustration someone is feeling, I hear the content of their message, and I reflect back what I see and hear. This helps me to clarify their real thoughts and feelings. It also helps me to stay focused. My success is directly proportionate to the long-term relationships that I build with my clients, other attorneys, and judges. It's crucial that I understand the people with whom I work in order to be successful.

"Speaking of success, I need to get back to work. While I'm finishing up a few things that need to be completed, think about what we can do to meet your goals for the day." Lonnie turned to her assistant to outline her day.

As Lonnie was finishing up, Alex remembered an important case she had been involved with last month. She'd been able to resolve a tense situation between two firmly-entrenched groups involving the use of land for a park. Each group was adamant as to where the park should be located, and the tension level had gone to the extreme. The two groups came together in the end, but Alex wondered how Lonnie ever got them to agree. This was the perfect time for him to get information from Lonnie about how to handle situations filled with conflict.

As Barbara was leaving the room, Alex asked, "About the case you had last month, Lonnie, how were you able to settle conflict about the final park location and have both groups in support of the decision?"

"Oh yes!" Lonnie rolled her eyes. "You must have read about the situation in the newspaper. The agreement of both groups to support the placement of the park had a lot to do with luck and the hard work of everyone involved. What specifically do you want to know?"

"Well, I'm beginning to learn from Smokey and my board that I may push my point too hard without considering the merits of the other side. I need to work on how not to get defensive when there is a disagreement. It's usually hard for me to reach an agreement with my sales representatives that we can both accept when our emotions are too high. I tend to become autocratic and tell them that we've had enough discussion, to just do it the way that I know is best." Alex rubbed his forehead.

"How were you able to get the two groups together and both committed to the solution?" he asked earnestly.

Lonnie summarized, "It was a long process, taking over twelve hours of working together, but I'll give you the *Reader's Digest* version. I strongly believe there must be a trusting relationship among all the people involved in a negotiation. In this case the two sides had never met. The first three hours we found out about each other, learned what our best hopes and worst fears were, established ground rules for how we would treat one another, outlined the desired goals, and identified the issues. The next seven hours we listened carefully as both sides explained their thoughts, feelings, and needs. The last couple of hours were used to reach an agreement that both groups could support."

Lonnie concluded, "The real challenge for me in those types of situations is to maintain my versatility. My job is to stay focused on keeping the emotions at a level where efforts will continue harmoniously toward resolving the situation. I had to listen carefully, making sure each side listened to the other. Once both sides felt they understood the other and recognized they both wanted the park, finalizing the placement, which met the goals both groups had established up front, assured there would be widespread support."

In long strides, Lonnie started for the door and said, "You can ask me other questions as we walk. I need to go to the fourth floor of the law library to meet with a law clerk about some research she's doing for me."

Alex hurried to catch up and asked, "What was the most important thing you learned from the park negotiation session?"

"Are you asking me what I think you could learn from that session, Alex?" Lonnie asked, smiling, with a twinkle in her eyes.

"Well, yes, I guess I'm asking that," Alex said in a surprised tone.

It's essential to know when to be firm and when to be gentle, making it possible for the interpersonal tension to be managed at a productive level, the task accomplished, and the people still committed.

"In situations like that I have to force myself and others to listen. It's difficult to listen and to understand truly the entire meaning of the message when emotions are so high. Keeping opposing groups focused isn't that difficult for me, but it takes effort! When people are highly involved, they often get off on their own stories. I have to bring them back gently to the subject without offending them. It's essential to know when to be firm and when to be gentle, making it possible for the interpersonal tension to be managed at a productive level, the task accomplished, and the people still committed," Lonnie said.

Lonnie and Alex arrived at the law library. As they walked through the rows of books and computers, Lonnie told Alex that the law clerk's name was Monica and that she was currently working for the firm before her second year in law school. Monica had been selected because of her outgoing personality. The firm wanted to groom her for employment with it after she graduated.

Upon entering a small office on the back wall, Lonnie introduced Alex to Monica. A smile brightened her face and Monica greeted Alex with a hearty handshake. She seemed young and looked more like an undergraduate student. Monica's style of dress was classic informal. She reminded Alex of a young Jacqueline Kennedy, with long brown hair, large dark eyes, and glasses perched on the top of her head. Without hesitation, Lonnie asked for an update on the progress of Monica's research.

Monica excitedly explained, "I found three cases from the district court that give us the information we need in order to deny the grievance being filed. In fact, with this information, our client has no obligation to the employee and can terminate immediately. I have the opinion already written for your review."

As Monica continued talking with a flourish of animation, Alex noticed that the length of Monica's explanation was irritating Lonnie. Monica was exploding with ideas about her research, totally unaware of Lonnie's mounting frustration level.

After three or four minutes, Lonnie snapped, "Monica, it's obvious you think you have this case analyzed and all the answers needed to settle it; however, I've not heard anything yet that would lead me to reach the same conclusion. I asked you for court decisions, not only from the district, but also from the appeals court and the Supreme Court. Where is the rest of the research?" Lonnie demanded, wearing an irritated look.

Monica was terribly quiet and looked as if she had just been kicked in the stomach. Her animation was gone, replaced by a sad dejected expression. She said, "I thought this was what you asked for, and I've tried to summarize the information and my thoughts for you. Isn't this what you wanted?"

Lonnie seemed to freeze. She realized that she had reacted too strongly and had hurt Monica. She regrouped and with a slight smile started again.

"You've done a lot of work. You believe your findings support our case, and they may; however, I need specific information on the three points I asked you to research. I'll then be able to decide on our strategy."

Alex was content to be on the sideline. He watched Lonnie as she clearly described what she wanted from Monica. Lonnie asked Monica to clarify what she thought her instructions were and asked if she could help start the research.

Monica cautiously replied, "No, I'm sure I understand exactly what you want. You want the citations, abstracts, and an objective summary of each case I find that is relevant to our research. I can complete the research now."

Lonnie complimented Monica on the research she had started with the district court, commenting on the good points that Monica had gathered. Lonnie then made a few suggestions on how to proceed. Lonnie concluded the conversation with a somewhat apologetic tone. "Monica, remember this work is part of your law education, and my role is to help you learn what you'll need to know in order to be successful as an attorney. I'm sorry I was abrupt. I may not have made myself as clear as I needed to with my original instructions to you."

Monica responded with a slight smile, "I appreciate your help. I probably didn't ask the questions I needed to ask in order to go ahead with the research. Talking has been helpful, though a little painful."

As Alex and Lonnie left the law library, they walked quietly for a few minutes. Finally Lonnie broke the silence.

"Well, I blew it with Monica. I felt frustrated and became impatient. Scenes like that used to happen frequently with me, until I realized that that style of behavior wasn't getting the results I needed or wanted. Law clerks and other attorneys in the firm used to cut me a wide path. They wouldn't stop to talk to me unless there was an urgent reason. That's when a partner in the law firm suggested that I meet Jan and Smokey. They helped me to understand that I could achieve optimal results by building effective relationships."

Lonnie added for emphasis, "When I became aware of how overbearing my actions came across to others, I realized why people avoided me or got into heated arguments with me. At the time, I was experiencing frustration because I was doing my own research and case preparation. I couldn't count on others to work the way I wanted. My tendency is to control people and what they do. Smokey helped me to realize that I could get better results if I focused on being clear with my expectations and let others, like Monica, have a say in how they do their jobs. Without the tension, my goals and the goals of others could both be met."

Alex laughed and said, "Your own *Ah Ha* about relationships, as Smokey would say."

"You're exactly right."

Lonnie's next meeting was at the Spencer Country Club with another attorney. They were meeting to play golf and to discuss a potential real estate transaction between their clients.

The attorney's name was Robert Wesley. He had been Lonnie's friend, socially and professionally, for the past fifteen years. Robert's client had property he thought Lonnie's client might want for future development.

Robert was a formidable figure at least six-feet six-inches tall and weighing close to three hundred pounds. His hair was red-blond; his eyes were kind. Alex noticed a trace of freckles across the bridge of his nose. Robert was dressed in a bright-red polo shirt and khaki shorts. He greeted Alex with a warm smile and a firm handshake.

Lonnie had earlier asked Robert's permission that Alex be allowed to accompany them while they golfed. Lonnie explained that Alex would be observing her as she interacted with others. With Alex's assurance of confidentiality, Robert graciously agreed to let him come along.

The sky was overcast and rain was predicted, but it hadn't dampened their spirits. Alex had long wondered how people conducted business on a golf course. He had never golfed. It took too much time, and he didn't mix play with work. He liked to meet with his clients in an office setting.

Before they approached the first tee, Lonnie asked for specific information on the commercial property that Robert was interested in selling. She said, "What makes your property something we should consider? The two pieces of property adjacent to my client's property will be for sale within the year. Also, your client's property is separated from ours by a road."

Robert seemed a bit surprised and said, "You get right to the point, don't you, Lonnie? I thought we might enjoy our game for at least a couple of holes before we began negotiating. When my client told me he was thinking about selling this particular piece of property, I immediately thought of you and your client. It would add to your client's opportunity for future business expansion."

"Undeveloped property in that area isn't selling for much now," Lonnie stated in a challenging tone as she hit her first ball straight down the fairway.

Robert didn't hit his first ball nearly as well as Lonnie; he hooked it into the rough. Alex decided that Robert seemed to be uncomfortable with the way the discussion was going, actually appearing to be relieved as he walked off alone.

As Lonnie and Robert hit onto the green, little was said between them. Lonnie looked as if she wanted to continue the discussion, but Robert seemed focused on his game and was strangely quiet.

As they walked to the second tee, Lonnie picked right up again. "What value, other than possible future expansion, do you believe the property would have for my client? The other two pieces of property are at least on the same side of the road."

Robert's face registered slight irritation. He tapped Lonnie on the elbow as he walked by and said, "Come on, Lonnie, my client's property is twice as big. Buying it would make sure no one boxes your client in." The next two holes were played in silence.

It was Robert who revived the conversation. He asked, "Lonnie, when is your daughter scheduled to leave for college?" Lonnie stopped and stood quietly, looking into the trees on the right, then straight down the fairway, as if she were carefully studying it. She spoke slowly as she placed her ball on the tee, "Julie is leaving for college a week from today. It's going to be hard to have her that far away, unable to see her again until Thanksgiving."

Alex was puzzled as Lonnie suddenly backed away from the discussion about the property. Lonnie let Robert take the lead in the conversation, and for the next fourteen holes they discussed their families and common problems in their law offices. Alex was beginning to wonder if Lonnie had forgotten why she was meeting with Robert. He was sure of one thing! A golf course was no place to conduct business.

Alex wondered why she wasn't pushing for a decision. She had been making strong points and had had Robert in a position where she was controlling the negotiations.

Just about the time Alex thought that Lonnie and Robert were discussing everything but the business at hand, Lonnie approached the topic of selling of the land. "Robert, can you tell me why your client wants to sell the land at this time?"

"Sure, he isn't in a hurry to sell, but he knows he never intends to develop it. His business is on the other side of town. He doesn't foresee a need for the land in the future. Since I know you and your client, I thought you might be interested."

"I appreciate you letting me know about it," Lonnie said with new warmth in her voice. "Tell me more about your client's timeline to sell and his asking price."

"Well, he wants a fair price for the property. He's willing to get two independent appraisals to see if a price can be agreed upon based on the estimates," Robert answered.

"That seems fair. Together, let's gather a list of appraisers to see if our clients can agree on two," Lonnie offered.

Robert agreed. They decided on a future timeline to have the appraisers named and the price set. This was completed by the eighteenth hole!

Alex was astonished. How had they moved from no action to an agreement so quickly and easily? Why had Lonnie stopped talking about the property for such a long time? How had they ended up discussing families and other unrelated topics?

As Lonnie drove back to the office, Alex began asking the questions that were buzzing around in his head.

"Why did the discussions go from the land purchase, to families, to a variety of other topics, and then back to the specifics on buying the land?"

Lonnie shook her head and said, "This is another case of my getting ahead of myself, of my not taking into account Robert's preferred interaction style. I've known Robert for years. I started off too fast, so I could meet my goals. I wanted the land at a fair price and I wanted to get business out of the way, so I could enjoy an afternoon of golf."

"'*Ah Ha!* I believe I'm beginning to understand, but please tell me, specifically, what you did and why?" Alex smiled, but his eyes were serious.

"Well, I know that Robert prefers an Amiable style of interaction with his clients. He's a hard bargainer and will always get the best for his clients; however, he negotiates based on the relationship he has with the person with whom he's working. I started out to meet my need for a quick decision on the deal. Robert wanted a decision just as much as I did, but he also wanted to begin with a firm foundation, by reestablishing our relationship.

"I noticed the tension Robert was feeling; he didn't want to deal with my questions. As I backed off, Robert relaxed and we renewed our trusting relationship. This was a crucial step for both of us, especially if we are to continue working together in the future." Lonnie emphasized this last part.

"Did you notice how quickly we came to an agreement, one good for both clients, after the relationship was affirmed?" Lonnie asked.

"Yes! And the deal seems like a fair one. Both clients will get what they want, or they can agree not to make a deal. It's evident now what happened, but I wouldn't have thought to ease up on my questions. I felt good about just being able to recognize the tension in Robert's voice as he walked off the first tee. How did you know to change the subject for a while?" Alex asked.

"You were more observant than I." Lonnie slowly shook her head. "At first I wasn't aware of Robert's discomfort; I kept pushing my points. When I noticed he was joking and trying to change the subject, I knew we wouldn't be able to work out a deal at that time.

"The tension was becoming high between us. I noticed that an edge of impatience had crept into Robert's voice. He didn't trust my motivation. A good working relationship is important for all of us, particularly for individuals with Robert's style of interaction. He needed to affirm that our interactions were honest and straightforward before we could begin.

"Successful negotiating attorneys establish and maintain good long-term relationships. It's a necessity because we work with one another many times over the years."

Alex sat heavily in his seat and began rubbing his forehead. He said, "I've never considered relationships to be an important part of the negotiation process. To me, negotiators just have to be hard-nosed, stick to their issues, and win." Now Alex was the one shaking his head.

"Do you think Robert would have come to me with the opportunity to make a deal for my client if he thought I would try to browbeat him?" Lonnie probed.

"Probably not. He would have first presented the deal to someone he trusted to be fair, and then maybe he would have given you a chance."

"Being tough and sticking to your issues doesn't mean you can't look for agreements where both parties will win. Knowing the other party's needs and searching for ways to meet those needs—as well as assuring that your needs are addressed—helps everyone to be a winner."

Lonnie completed her thought. "Everything is connected. If I were to have talked Robert into meeting my client's offering price without considering Robert's client's needs, they might hold out for a financing package that wouldn't work for my client. . Besides, in the future, I'll be working with Robert, his clients, and friends of his clients many times; thus, it's important to keep a good working relationship."

> I can be more effective and better meet my goals if I help others to reach their goals.

As Alex was getting out of Lonnie's car and preparing to leave, he said, "Lonnie, this day has been much more than I expected. I believe that my style of interaction with people is much like yours, but you certainly are more versatile than I am. I can see how I might cause people to be uncomfortable with my straightforward style of interaction. More importantly, I see that I can be more effective and better meet my goals if I help others to reach their goals.

"Watching you adjust, when needed, as you've talked to people, amazes me. You truly care about people and about what you're trying to accomplish."

Lonnie carefully phrased her words. "Thank you for your insights and your comments on how I work. It isn't easy. An *"Ah Ha"* that I've learned over time that has helped me the most is that being versatile in relationships is the most important quality I'll need to ensure future success, to take action, so both people can gain as a result of the interaction."

"Thanks, Lonnie. I have a lot to talk over with Smokey," Alex said, as he started to close the car door.

"Oh, one more thing I learned today! There can be a win/win deal negotiated while golfing, but when you golf, you play to win," Alex said with a big smile.

PUTTING IT ALL TOGETHER

Versatility is demonstrated when
both you and the other person gain
as a result of the interaction
between you.
—Gerald L. Prince

Alex was at Smokey's office before eight the next morning. Smokey's assistant, Christine, took Alex into the office and brought him some coffee. Christine was slender and had a warm smile that reached her eyes. Smokey told Alex that they would meet for part of the morning and would need a comfortable place to spread out.

Smokey's office was comfortable with a cheerful red-and-blue checked carpet. There was a round work table at one end, with comfortable leather chairs surrounding it. Smokey's desk faced a large picture window, looking out over rolling green hills. Robert Lynne Nelson prints of Hawaiian ocean scenes hung on the walls between a writing board on one wall and storyboards on the other walls. All in all, it was a spacious and inviting room.

Soon after Alex was seated, Smokey arrived and warmly greeted him. "Alex, it's good to see you! You've had quite a time over the last few days. I'm anxious to hear what you've learned now that you've completed your visits. Let's begin by reviewing the two questions I asked you to find answers for during each visit to a board member. Tell me about the four people on your board of directors. Describe in detail their styles of interaction and how you would interact effectively with each one."

Alex shivered and courageously began. "Well, being with Rachel Williams was like being with a whirlwind. She moved around the office quickly and always seemed to be involved with people. She had a boatload of ideas on how to improve her animal hospital; she talked constantly. I'm not sure if she followed through with all of her ideas. She was emotionally overwhelming at times. I see her preferred style of interaction as Expressive.

"Greg Drydon was interesting to observe. He seemed genuinely to like kids, teachers, and parents. He displayed tremendous patience as he worked through a variety of difficult situations. His relationships with his staff were positive; they worked well together as a team. There was some trouble handling tension and conflict. Once a decision was made, he took a lot of time getting started." Alex hesitated, and then proudly offered, "His style of interaction seems to be Amiable.

"Jim Watson really knew his antiques business and the entire inventory in his shop. I haven't seen anyone who could describe a lamp right down to the blemishes on the base as Jim did. When it came to details and organization, he was right on target. In one case, he provided more information than his clients wanted or needed, and that almost cost him a sale. When he interacted with clients who expressed themselves in feelings, he needed to put forth an extra effort rather than communicating facts. Jim told me that his preferred style of interaction is Analytical.

"Lonnie Phillips was like you and me, Smokey. She got things done quickly and got right to the point. Lonnie told it as she saw it. If I worked with her, I would know where I stood. She had high expectations for what she considered to be acceptable work. Sometimes, it appeared as if she ran over people. She had to work hard to let others know she listened to them, because she was so fast-acting. I liked her preferred style of interaction. It would probably be what you would call a Driving style."

Smokey said, "Alex, I'm truly impressed at how hard you've worked to understand the different styles of interaction and how accurately you're able to describe the effects of each style." Smokey beamed with satisfaction. "Now, tell me how you personally would work effectively with each member of your board of directors. What 'Ah Ha's' have you learned?"

Alex enthusiastically responded, "Smokey, when you first said Relationships, relationships, relationships, that is all there is: are relationships,' I couldn't fathom what you meant. I've always focused on the bottom line, the profit. After my recent experiences and the feedback I've received, that saying takes on a new significance.

> If I'm to be an effective manager rather than just an efficient manager, I need to communicate more appropriately with people.

"A big 'Ah Ha' that I've discovered is that if I'm to be an effective manager rather than just an efficient manager, I need to communicate more appropriately with people. I need to interact with people in a way that they understand and appreciate." Alex thoughtfully added, "Mutual understanding is partly based on my interaction style, but far more important is my versatility. And this is powerful! I can enhance a relationship and be a more successful communicator by focusing on other's needs first and then my needs.

"Realizing that other people see my preferred style of interaction as Driving, I need to control my areas of weakness and to recognize and understand others' preferred interaction style. Then I need to focus on interacting with them in their style. It's a shock to know that people can view my behavior as cold, abrupt, or rough. I do care about people. It's just that I only need to receive and to give the information that will be needed to get things done quickly, keeping focused on the business at hand."

Smokey was wearing a huge smile! "Now, tell me about each board member and what you would need to do in order to be an effective supervisor with each one."

"Well," Alex started, "when working with a person like Lonnie, I would need to show results, agree on goals, and allow her the freedom to work within the limits agreed upon. I would need to support her conclusions and help to generate ideas to further implement her plans. If I disagreed with her, I would have to be firm and connect my objections to the agreed upon goals. She would appreciate being commended for her performance on the results attained."

Alex intently looked at Smokey's face for any sign that he was on the right track and then forged ahead. "Lonnie would work best if she received a percentage of the sale or a bonus based on her productivity. Because I have a Driving style of interaction, Lonnie would appreciate my ability to make decisions and my fast pace, though she could still view me as being bossy, tough, and unfeeling.

"Being versatile with the other styles of interaction is more difficult for me, but I'm learning.

"If I correctly understand the Analytical style of interaction, I would work best with Jim by appreciating his fact orientation and his logical and objective approach to planning and solving problems. It would be important to support his principles and his thorough processing of problems.

"To be effective as Jim's manager, I would want to show an understanding of the information he collects and not too quickly jump to a solution or offer help. If I feel his decision isn't right, I would need to be accurate with my information as I presented my thoughts. It would be important that I demonstrate an understanding of his point of view and provide an organized, well thought out, systematic presentation of my position. I would attempt to recognize him for his planning, his thoroughness, and for his follow-through as he met his sale's goals. Jim would appreciate my efficiency, my interest in data, and my task-orientation, but he might be troubled by my fast pace, my competitiveness, and my willingness to take risks." Alex hesitated. Then he admitted, "Greg's Amiable style of interaction is the hardest style for me to understand. I have to admit that I have very few ideas as to how I would work effectively with him."

"Alex, that doesn't surprise me," Smokey inserted. "Greg's Amiable style of interaction is basically the most different style from your Driving style. It will be difficult for you not to judge what you do and don't like about the Amiable style of interaction. Consider this question. Was Greg effective with the people he dealt with throughout the day?"

"Yes, absolutely! I couldn't have put up with all the petty wants, questions and demands that he faced."

"Did Greg use an Amiable style of interaction with each and every person he met with?" Smokey asked, knowing the answer.

"No. Not at all. He seemed to adjust and to do just the right thing to reach all the decisions he had to make, in the parent conferences, and in his feedback to the teachers." Alex was surprised at his own answer.

Smokey said, "It sounds to me as if Greg used his versatility to meet the needs of each person, individually, thereby developing mutually productive relationships." Smokey waited for a response from Alex.

> It's not so much the style of interaction; it's the versatility that makes good relationships!

"Another '*Ah Ha!*' That's right. It's not so much the style of interaction, it's the versatility that makes good relationships! So, even if the Amiable style of interaction is hard for me to understand, I can still be effective with those who prefer that style. I just need to be versatile," Alex concluded. Then he continued, "Well, then, if I'm to be effective with those who have an Amiable style, like Greg, they would appreciate concern about them as individuals. It would be important to show a sincere interest in their families, to be willing to slow down and to take the time to develop relationships as we worked to accomplish our goals. I should take the time to understand their personal goals, to find a common ground where we can connect our goals.

"It could be difficult for me, but in order to be effective, I would need to be patient and to encourage discussion in a non-threatening environment. I could best recognize Greg by giving him a warm personal thanks and maybe by taking him to lunch. He would appreciate my efficiency and discipline, but he may have trouble with my fast action, risk taking, and unfeeling bottom line orientation." Alex gave an enormously audible sigh and waited nervously for Smokey's feedback.

"That's a good start as you attempt to work more effectively with the Amiable style of interaction. You'll need to keep thinking about ways to stretch your versatility in order to meet the needs of an Amiable," Smokey stressed.

Alex could see that Smokey was waiting patiently for him to continue. He wondered if he looked as drained as he felt? He said, "Those individuals who have Rachel's Expressive style of interaction would appreciate my support for their ideas, dreams, and intuitions, and my fast pace. They would find it important that I take time to explore mutually interesting projects and thoughts with them.

"The Expressive's opinions are important to them, and I need to let them express themselves. Details may not be as important to them. It would be best to help them to build plans of action with details. It's important to recognize the Expressive individual quickly, personally, and publicly. Rachel would like my independence and decisiveness. However, she could find my style of interaction to be difficult because of my serious no-nonsense approach and my lack of personal warmth.

"Rachel's Expressive style of interaction would be a challenge. I would be enthralled with the fast paced exciting environment, but her lack of organization would be frustrating for me," Alex confessed.

> "…your comment tells me more about you and your versatility, than it tells me about Rachel."

"Alex, you might be surprised to know that your comment tells me more about you and your versatility than it tells me about Rachel." Alex shrugged, feeling somewhat uneasy, and asked, "What do you mean?"

"Was Rachel aware of where things were kept in her clinic?" Smokey asked.

"Yes, she seemed to know where everything was, but her shelves could have been labeled, her books categorized, and work schedules completed in a timelier manner." Alex was defending his position.

Smokey earnestly asked, "Is the need for orderliness your need? If Rachel and the animal hospital are able to operate effectively, meeting and exceeding their clients' needs, whose method of organization is right? Often our style of interaction influences our judgments, but it won't help another person with a different style to work more effectively. Does this make sense, Alex?"

"Right between the eyes," Alex said with astonishment. "I want everyone to act like me. The way I do things makes perfectly good sense to me, and I've always thought everyone else viewed the world the same way I do. It's really an 'Ah Ha' for me to discover that others feel that the way they act and think is just as logical to them as my actions and thoughts are to me. There is more than one way to be right; my way isn't the only right way."

Smokey looked like a proud papa. "You're truly starting to understand versatility. Always keep in mind that versatility is effectively managing the tension of an interpersonal relationship in order to keep the interaction productive. Versatility allows you to manage the feelings and to achieve the results you seek."

Alex interrupted, "What about my tension? If I'm managing others' tension, what happens to my tension when the sales quotas aren't met and the clients aren't contacted?"

Smokey answered Alex's question with a question. "How did Lonnie make sure that the intended goals were reached and still effectively manage the tension of her clients?"

Alex had to reach back into his memory. Lonnie had been able to reach a deal with Robert while on the golf course, but only after adjusting her style of interaction to deal effectively with Robert's feelings. She had to work on the relationship first.

Alex also vividly recalled the incident when Lonnie became impatient with Monica, the young law clerk. Lonnie was able to manage and to repair the tension that she had created in the relationship only when she listened to Monica's ideas and when she clarified and redirected Monica with specific instructions as to how to proceed.

"*AH HA!*" An idea struck like lightning! He thought, "I bet that Monica's preferred style of interaction is Expressive."

"I could use a Coke!" Alex said out loud, as if he deserved a reward for his efforts. He grinned widely and laughed softly as Smokey stepped into the hall to tell Christine that they were in need of a couple of Cokes. Christine arrived quickly with the Coke Alex had requested, classic, little ice.

After two large gulps, Alex was ready to share his ideas with Smokey. He thoughtfully began, "In both incidents, Lonnie and the other person each achieved his or her goals. Lonnie adjusted her style of interaction in each situation, thereby managing her tension, along with the other's tension; she used the styles model to enhance and to receive positive results."

Smokey said, smiling broadly, "Now that's what I call versatility! Lonnie put forth the effort to make the relationships mutually beneficial for both."

"Smokey," Alex said, "you and my board of directors have turned my world upside down. It's much clearer now for me to be able to realize that people think in other ways than I do. This new way of thinking gives me the tools, the pieces to the puzzle that will help me to meet successfully the needs of my staff and my clients, reducing stress and tension for all. I'll treat them the way they prefer to be treated.

> The key is versatility; to be successful, I must be versatile!

"An amazingly, huge '*Ah Ha*' that I discovered is that each style has strengths and weaknesses. It doesn't matter as much what my preferred style of interaction is. The key is versatility; to be successful, I must be versatile."

"Excellent insight, Alex," Smokey said, as he pushed out of his chair. "Now, as I mentioned earlier, I have a lot of writing to do. We'll need to continue this conversation in the morning."

"Great, I'm worn out. Making sense of all of this is a struggle. Breaking at this point will allow me to review what we've talked about and attempt to put it all together," Alex said as he stood to leave.

"Looking at relationships, using this different frame of reference, is difficult. It's exciting, though, to become aware that we hold the key to positive outcomes, not only for ourselves, but also for others. I want to see you first thing in the morning. We'll finish up our discussion then," Smokey said. He was limping as he crossed the floor to open the door for Alex.

ALEX'S "Ah Ha's"

A person's greatest hope
is to be understood.
—Stephen R. Covey

Alex and Linda had been up a good part of the night sitting at the kitchen table, sharing coffee and ideas about what Alex had experienced and what he had learned.

They made a game out of writing the names of individuals they both knew on small file cards, discussing the behaviors that they felt each person generally displayed, and then placing the names in appropriate piles: Expressive, Amiable, Driver, Analytical. Each person earned extra points if he or she had been known to show versatility. Both realized, given their limited knowledge, there was a huge margin for error, but it was fun!

Alex was up with the chickens, as the saying goes, and off to meet Smokey at his office. He was excited to get to work with his newly found knowledge.

As Smokey greeted Alex in the outer office, he could see that Alex was bursting with energy. Alex began talking immediately as he lowered himself into his favorite chair in Smokey's office.

"All this information about building and maintaining relationships is foreign to me. I've always thought that getting the job done was all that counted. Now I'm beginning to see the importance of not only building, but also maintaining good relationships with the people I work with and manage, if my goal is for long-term success. I always knew it was important to have good relationships with the customer. It didn't occur to me that my colleagues and sales representatives are my customers too."

Smokey smiled. "As a supervisor, it's even more important for you to treat your staff well because they tend to treat customers as they are treated. You're the model for customer relationships. Your staff looks to you for what is expected as they interact with customers. The base of any effective relationship is trust on both the professional and the personal level."

"How do I get my staff to trust me?" Alex asked.

"The way you develop trust with your staff is by creating interaction where honest listening and open communication are encouraged without fear. The result will be better decisions, plans, and productivity, because you're all working together for joint success. Everyone contributes, and no one holds back." Smokey's eyes were serious as he spoke.

They must know that you're working for their success.

Smokey continued, "I recently read a book, *Whale Done*, about the trainers at the Sea World Parks. They have certain methods to train the whales and dolphins. The first thing they do is build a trusting relationship between the marine mammals and themselves. They jump into the water and swim with the whales and dolphins until the mammals are convinced the trainers mean them no harm. Before you can be effective in working with your staff, you need to prove to them that you mean them no harm. They must know that you're working for their success."

Alex said, "I can just imagine what my sales staff at Rivonia Technology thought of the way I interacted with them. No wonder the representatives were requesting transfers to other regions. I managed them as I was managed. Nowadays people won't take the grief that I caused my staff. The saying around the office was that Alex will never get ulcers; he just gives them to everyone else. I was inept as a manager, but I didn't know it. I've experienced and learned so much in these past few days. I'm ready to do a better job." Alex spoke with conviction.

"It sounds to me as if all the thinking and putting things back together that you've been working on is starting to make sense. Review with me what you've learned about becoming a better manager." Smokey requested as he leaned back in his chair and put on his listening face.

"The new knowledge I have about versatility and your 'Ah Ha's' on understanding the styles of the interaction model will be a lifesaver for me. If I can apply half of what I've learned, I'm sure that in my next job I'll be more effective with my staff. I've experienced invaluable 'Ah Ha's' for effective relationships. When you first said, 'Relationships relationships, relationships, relationships, that is all there is: are relationships,' I had no idea what you were trying to tell me. I've discovered that good relationships bring about better sales and more money. When the relationships are productive, people enjoy their work and enjoy working with each other. The added bonus is that we also become better spouses and parents. Smokey, I'd like to share a few of my 'Ah Ha's.'"

"Here goes," Alex thought, taking a deep breath.

> Productive relationships are all about balance, meeting the needs of everyone involved. It isn't a case of either/or, but of both.

"Productive relationships are all about balance, meeting the needs of everyone involved. It isn't a case of either/or, but of both. The Chinese proverb you have displayed on your desk carries incredible significance. 'Seek not to know all the answers, but to understand the questions.' If I am to succeed, and I know now that I will, I need to seek sincerely to understand the other person. That person will then usually seek to understand me and together we'll come up with a better solution. People who feel that their ideas and feelings are heard, appreciated, and understood become part of the solution. They become committed and take ownership for the desired success.

"I was amazed to learn that over ninety-percent of communication is nonverbal. From now on, I'll carefully watch the facial expressions, the tone of voice, the pace of speech, and other nonverbal clues.

"I control only fifty percent of a relationship, but what I do with my part can make the relationship productive and satisfying for both of us.

"Versatility isn't something you do to others; it's something you do to yourself.

"Versatility is evident, when the relationship brings out the best in each person.

"Changing relationships begins with me.

"I get a feeling that those are just the beginning of my *'Ah Ha's.'*" Alex finished with a loud laugh and a proud smile.

"You've gained immensely from your experiences with your board members," Smokey praised Alex's efforts. "Now the challenge is to put your learning into practice." Then he added, "Speaking of practice, Jan called earlier and has some thoughts about your next step for getting a job. She's a talented person, yet I can tell you don't think much of her efforts to help you."

"You're right. I feel that she's been too slow in helping me move toward a new career," Alex acknowledged.

"Let's see, you're unhappy with Jan's snail pace, and you're disappointed with your progress. And yet you're excited with your new knowledge, and you realize that this knowledge is a lifeline you need in order for you to better work with others. You now hold the key to effective relationships," Smokey said, with eyes twinkling.

"Let's back up a little and apply what you've learned. What role did Jan play in moving you toward these new insights?" Smokey asked.

"Let's see. Jan asked a ton of questions. She is precise in her actions and in what she wants and expects. She works at a slow pace. Her preferred style of interaction could be on the Analytical side, though she doesn't seem to be versatile. She didn't pick up on the fast pace that I prefer or arrange for even one job interview," Alex replied, becoming well aware that he was missing the point.

"Think, Alex," Smokey said emphatically. "Jan was direct with you. Through her insightful study, she knew you needed additional skills in order to be successful in any job. You couldn't accept her ideas, yet she designed the exact strategy that got your attention. Jan methodically chose each individual that was to be on your board, those individuals who could best help you to understand and to achieve the essential skills you needed. Jan hooked you up with me, and I was direct and fastpaced enough, wasn't I?"

"Yes! My board of directors experience opened the door for me to move ahead successfully in all areas of my life," Alex sincerely responded. "Watching Greg and Rachel interact with their clients, yet still get the job done, gave me an appreciation for their styles of interaction. I used to label people like Greg and Rachel as touchy-feely. To observe each member of my board as he or she interacted and adjusted their styles with clients was life-altering for me. Each client had a preferred style of interaction, yet the goals were successfully reached, and the relationships were enriched.

"Lonnie and Rachel helped me to understand that controlling others' actions is not the best way to get the job done, especially for long-term results. Sometimes a slower pace is actually faster. Of course, I understand and like the Driving style of interaction best. Lonnie uses a Driving style of interaction. She gets the job done and fast. Yet, using her versatility, she supports and encourages the people she works with toward success.

"Smokey, you and the rest of my board definitely got my attention, introducing me to the importance of the Platinum Rule. Jan did meet my needs," Alex said as he sat back in his chair, chuckling and shaking his head. "I believe I do owe her an apology; I gave her a pretty hard time. I sincerely appreciate that you shared the style interaction model for your 'Ah Ha's' with me, helping me to discover 'Ah Ha's' of my own."

Smokey said, "I've enjoyed our discussions, and I'll look forward to seeing you again. You know, we're still your board, unless you replace us with other members. Remember, Alex, versatility is something you must consistently and tenaciously work on each and every day. You may need our help to stay on track with your new skills. Being versatile is hard in ordinary times—much harder when you're under pressure."

Alex left Smokey's office with mixed feelings. He was looking forward to working again. He knew he had experienced an extraordinary opportunity. Now he needed to begin this challenge, to use his new skills and attitudes. It was exhilarating to have worked with people who cared enough to work for his success.

With his hands buried deep in his jacket pockets, Alex walked down the stairs and toward his car. He had always thought of himself as having all the answers. He wasn't so sure anymore.

Alex's thoughts turned to his family. What would his new skills and discoveries mean to them? He was surprised as he realized that this was the first time he'd seriously considered how his past actions had impacted his family. What had his interactions been like with Linda, Mitch, and Stephanie?

Deep in thought, Alex sat quietly in his car and reviewed some of his actions. He thought, "Basically, I need to try harder at home to consider my family, to use the interaction skills I've learned. I imagine Linda, Mitch, and Stephanie probably see me in the same light as the people at work. Wow, that's not what I want. It's time for a change. I need to apply my new skills to each and every area of my life!"

> Wow, that's not what I want. It's time for a change.

When dinner was over, Alex asked everyone to stay at the kitchen table so he could update them about his job search experiences. His progress report was quick; Stephanie and Mitch had homework, and Linda needed to telephone the parents of one of her students.

Alex shared with them that he had learned a few important things that would help him in a new job, but more important was the fact that his new insights would help him to be a better father and husband.

After his family left the table, Alex sat quietly. A smile spread from the corner of his mouth, extending from ear to ear. He decided that he could better explain things to his family through his actions, not his words.

THE NEXT CHALLENGES: PERSONALLY AND PROFESSIONALLY

Value the different interaction styles,
respect the needs of each style,
work for open communication,
and success will occur.
—Gerald L. Prince

Alex was still on an emotional high when he arrived at Jan's office. He couldn't help himself. He felt invigorated with his newfound knowledge and could hardly wait to tell Jan about his *"Ah Ha's."*

Jan's first appointment was running a few minutes over, and Alex thought about how he would have reacted two weeks earlier. The old Alex's normal response would have been impatience and sarcastic remarks about his time being as valuable as Jan's time.

Alex decided to try a new and—he hoped—a more versatile approach with Jan to see if he could apply what he had learned. He observed Jan when she came out of her office and tried to determine how her day was going.

Jan hurried past everyone in the waiting room. Alex sized up the situation and greeted her. "You look like you're under some pressure. Could you use a little time to collect yourself before our meeting?"

Jan looked surprised and wearily brushed her hand over her forehead. "Why, yes, Alex, I do need just a few minutes to get some things taken care of, and then I'll be able to give you my full attention."

Jan made a quick phone call and gave her assistant instructions on writing a letter that needed to be delivered immediately. She walked over to the water fountain and took a long drink, a deep breath, and walked back to Alex.

"Alex, please come into my office. I've talked to Smokey several times since you left, and I'm anxious to hear from you about your discoveries," Jan said as they walked into her office.

Alex was focusing on using his new skills. He felt that Jan's preferred style of interaction was probably the Analytical style or, maybe Amiable. He knew that this would be a good time to continue recognizing Jan's tensions and to attempt to apply what he had learned.

Alex was facing a dilemma. Should he interact with Jan as if she preferred an Analytical style of interaction or an Amiable style? He thought a second and then responded with a reply that he thought would consider both styles. He reasoned that Jan's response would tell him more about which style she preferred.

"Jan, you appear more relaxed now, but still preoccupied." Alex held his breath, waiting for her response.

"It's a hectic time for the entire office right now. The news is all good. Quarterly reports are due, and our client load is increasing faster than we can find good career counselors to help us. I just need more hands to take care of all the details," Jan replied. "Thanks for noticing. I didn't know my stress level was so obvious."

Alex quickly considered Jan's response. He felt sure that Jan's preferred style of interaction was Analytical. She appeared to focus more on organization and details than on her feelings.

Although his actions felt stilted and somewhat mechanical, Alex knew that he was making an important first step. How could he help this meeting to be productive for both of them?

Jan pulled her chair close to the table. "Now, Alex, I'm anxious to know. Were your visits with the members of your board positive experiences? Do you feel that you discovered some new skills that will be beneficial to you as you enter the job market? What are some of the most important ideas that you discovered?"

Alex sat quietly, thinking before he responded. What he was about to say would be difficult for him, but it needed to be said. He started slowly. "Jan, I owe you an apology for the way I acted about the help you were giving me. I judged you from my style of interaction with others, and I wasn't open to any type of change. In the past few weeks, I've been through so many life-changing experiences. You're the one who made it possible. Thank you."

"Alex, thank you. My satisfaction comes from seeing how you've taken the responsibility for your own learning. I'm proud of the tremendous effort you've made toward becoming a more positive thoughtful person. You've worked hard to understand and to achieve the skills that you needed to be an effective supervisor."

Alex sincerely continued, "While we're talking about this, I feel sure that Linda, my wife, and my two kids, Mitch and Stephanie, would want me to thank you too. The skills that I've learned will be beyond value to our family, creating a more positive and a more productive family.

"Jan, I have a long way to go before I'll be as versatile as you or each member of my board or Smokey. But I now know what I have to do to become successful—not only as a manager but also as a person.

"It's now obvious that in the past I haven't done a good job of understanding people. I have a long way to go and many new skills that I need to master. I need to make adjustments in the way that I interact with and manage others. As a supervisor, I thought it was my responsibility to treat each person the same and to expect the same results from each one. During the past two weeks, I've learned that people think and learn differently, and that isn't bad or good. We can think differently, yet work toward the same goals and still get the job done.

> Treating people the way that they understand best—in the style that they prefer—makes a lot more sense than treating everyone the same.

"Becoming aware of the different preferred styles of interaction will help me to understand the needs of those individuals I'll be working with. I've come to appreciate how differences can actually help in making better and more productive decisions. The key is my versatility. If I can remain versatile, I can utilize the different points of view to develop divergent approaches for creative solutions. Treating people the way that they understand best—in the style that they prefer—makes a lot more sense than treating everyone the same.

"This is the first time that I've considered the idea of people having opinions that differ from mine as positive. As a supervisor I often just dismissed their ideas when sales representatives raised objections or proposed different strategies. I'm sure I missed out on many good ideas and kept other good ideas from even being offered out of fear of what I would say. I can see now why my sales representatives were not committed to my plans and requested transfers to other regions. People need to feel that what they do at work makes a difference. I wasn't even aware that there was a problem.

"Jan, thank you for setting me up with my board of directors and with Smokey. Rachel, Greg, Jim, and Lonnie were great. They helped me to see how each interaction style can be effective. Their versatility showed me that relationships can and need to be good for me and the people I deal with each day. I appreciate the opportunity you gave me to work with Smokey. He's a remarkable person; he gave freely of himself to help me to understand and gain a whole basket of '*Ah Ha's*' about relationships. The Platinum Rule will be of service to me in any job I may get. Your plan was extremely insightful, creative, and exactly what I needed. I wasn't sure where Smokey was going with all those surveys, but I understand now. It's crucial that I work to achieve results that are beneficial to each person in every interaction, to work for the success of my customers, my colleagues, the company, and me."

> Versatility isn't always easy, but it's well worth the effort.

Alex said with an unusual display of emotion, "You are the catalyst for all that I've learned. My passion for wanting to do my very best has returned. It's a great feeling to look forward to going back to work."

Jan was impressed and surprised at the drastic change she saw in Alex. "Thank you, Alex. Giving compliments and thanking people is something I don't do enough of either. I'm continuing to learn more about versatility every day as I work to meet the individual's needs in different situations. Versatility isn't always easy, but it's well worth the effort."

"These last few weeks have been a whirlwind. I've been on the go constantly, learned and thought so much that I'm ready for a vacation," Alex said.

"Not so fast, Alex! There are some exciting job opportunities I want to talk over with you."

EPILOGUE

Success is not something that
others can give you.
—John Wooden

A message to you from Alex:

The experience with my board of directors has been a real eye-opener for me. I didn't realize that other people saw the world differently than I did. Learning to communicate with them in the way they can best understand now seems so logical, but it is still going to be hard to do consistently.

As important as this learning experience was for me, I hope you have gained from it too. Watching the members of my board of directors made me aware that, as effective as they were, they were still learning about versatility and how to be more productive in their interactions. Smokey and my board members taught me to be aware of the needs of others and of the situations during my interactions with people. I need to take this understanding and act appropriately so everyone wins.

All people struggle with developing effective relationships. Improving versatility is meant for everyone seeking to be a better person and professional. I will have to continue to work on being more versatile in each important relationship every day of my life.

Linda, my wife, said that improving her versatility would be a tremendous help to her as a teacher. It continues to help each one of the members of my board of directors in their lives. Whether a person is a sales manager, educator, supervisor, lawyer, parent—most any occupation—success depends on being effective with others. It is a lifelong process!

I hope, by sharing my story, you can gain some ideas for a more productive and satisfying life.

Now, I would like to share with you some of the *"Ah Ha's"* I gained about versatility.

- We create tension by assuming our expectations are obvious, understood, and shared by the other person.

- Versatility occurs when the relationship brings out the best in each person.

- Understanding the styles of others helps us to appreciate the differences.

- If we don't understand behavior, we often judge it as wrong.

- Intellectual maturity is the ability to see another person's point of view.

- Versatility isn't self-less or self-ish behavior, but it is self-ful. It is an effective interaction that is mutually beneficial to both individuals. It is working together and gaining from the synergy.

- Reflective listening is an essential skill for versatility. Listening requires patience and emotional strength to focus on another person's message.

- Reflective listening is a risk. It takes personal security to be able to listen without judgment. You open yourself up to be influenced and to be changed. As a result of increasing your listening ability, you will have more influence because the other person knows you have understood.

- The outcome of versatility is the ability to understand another person's point of view, to know your issues, and work effectively to meet the needs of each person.

- Value the differences, and synergy will occur from the respect and communication.

- When you listen to really understand, you may find there is a tremendous difference in perceptions.

- Great communication is not effective because of the technique; it is effective because of your passion to build productive relationships.

- Remember: "Versatility is not an act; it's a habit practiced every day.

Best wishes on your journey,
ALEX

ABOUT THE AUTHOR

Education

Gerald Prince has been a public school teacher, counselor, principal, and central office administrator. He has been the director of personnel, planning, and evaluation, assistant superintendent, and director of teaching and learning. In addition, he has taught courses for over a dozen universities from Hawaii to New York.

Business

Prince has served as a consultant and conducted seminars with veterinarians, physicians, attorneys, hotel executives, insurance executives, accounting firms, and other business people. He has designed and provided programs for improving human interactions followed up with individual coaching sessions for the development of in-depth leadership skills.

Speaking and Publishing

Prince has conducted seminars and consulted with schools and businesses throughout the United States and Canada. The programs have focused on developing skills in planning, leadership, emotional intelligence, building a culture, communications, and related areas. He has been a speaker at numerous national, state, and local conferences on a variety of topics for improving the interaction between people to increase productivity. Prince has been the author of numerous articles and programs on a wide range of topics regarding people skills and professional development.

Personal

Prince's bachelor's and master's degrees are from Brigham Young University and his doctorate is from the University of Northern Colorado. He is a continual learner and has participated in courses and through personal experience in leadership, conflict resolution, systems approaches to change, creative thinking, human interaction, and many other areas. He lives with his wife, Barbara, and has two grown children, Kami and Kortnee, and one grandson, Atticus.

RESOURCES

For additional information on the Interaction Styles programs or other programs contact:

Dr. Gerald L. Prince
Prince Ventures
6854 Kilt Court
Worthington, Ohio 43085
614-888-3226
glprince@aol.com

Effectiveness Institute
2249 152nd Avenue N.E.
Redmond, Washington 98052
800-805-8654

TRACOM Corporation
8878 South Barron Blvd.
Highlands Ranch, Colorado 80129
800-221-2321

OTHER READINGS TO DISCOVER YOUR OWN "Ah Ha's"

Blanchard, K. *(2002). Whale Done: The Power of Positive Relationships*. New York: The Free Press.

Block, P. (1987). *The Empowered Manager:* San Francisco: Jossey-Bass Publishers.

Bowman, L. G. & Deal, T. E. (1995). *Leading With Soul*. San Francisco: Jossey-Bass. Publishers.

Buckingham, M. & Coffman, C. (1999). *First, Break All the Rules*. New York: Simon & Schuster.

Buckingham, M. & Clifton, D. O. (2001). *Now, Discover Your Strengths*. New York: The Free Press.

Covey, S. R. (1989). *The Seven Habits of Highly Effective People*. New York: Simon & Schuster, Inc.

Covey, S. R. (2004). *The 8th Habit: From Effectiveness to Greatness*. New York: Free Press.

Goleman, D. *Primal Leadership*. (2002). Boston: Harvard Business School Press.

Harvey, E. L. & Lucia, A. D. (1993). *Walk The Talk...and Get the Results You Want*. Dallas: Performance Systems Corporation.

Hitt, W. D. *The Model Leader: A Fully Functioning Person*. (1993). Columbus: Battelle Press.

Lee, B. *The Power Principle: Influence With Honor*. (1997). New York: Simon & Schuster, Inc.

Merrill, D. & Reid, R. (1981). *Personal Style and Effective Performance*. Radnor: Chilton Book Company.

Pattakos, A. *Prisoners of Our Thoughts*. (2004). Berrett-Koehler Publishers, Inc.

Wheatley, M. J. (1999). *Leadership and the New Science*. San Francisco Berrett-Koehler Publishers.

978-0-595-36440-4
0-595-36440-3